Alive with Jesus

a Junior High Bible Study Collection

Concordia Publishing House

Copyright © 2008 Concordia Publishing House
3558 S. Jefferson Ave., St. Louis, MO 63118-3968
1-800-325-3040 • www.cph.org

All rights reserved. Unless specifically noted, no part of this publication may be reproduced, stored in a retrieval system, or transmitted, in any form or by any means, electronic, mechanical, photocopying, recording, or otherwise, without the prior written permission of Concordia Publishing House.

The purchaser of this publication is allowed to reproduce the marked portions contained herein for classroom use. These resources may not be transferred or copied to another user.

Portions originally published by Concordia Publishing House, copyright © 1999, 2000, 2001, 2002, 2003, 2004.

Written by Kurt Bickel, Julie Cohrs, Tom Couser, Bill Cullen, Chris Drager, Bianca Elliott, Jim Elsner, Mark Etter, Heidi Fingerlin, Gretchen Gebhardt, John Hagge, Kirk Hille, Roger Howard, Lisa Keyne, Beth Murphy, Max Murphy, John Nunes, Craig Parrott, Craig Patterson, Daniel Pfaffe, Jay Reed, Christine Ross, Matthew Schaefer, Barney Schroeder, Byron Schroeder, Rebecca Spitzack, Julie Steigemeyer, Cindy Twillman, Susan Voss, Malinda Walz, and Karen Westbrooks.

Edited by Mark S. Sengele

Scripture quotations are taken from the HOLY BIBLE, NEW INTERNATIONAL VERSION®. NIV®. Copyright © 1973, 1978, 1984 by International Bible Society. Used by permission of Zondervan Publishing House. All rights reserved.

Your comments and suggestions concerning the material are appreciated. Please write to the Editor of Youth Materials, Concordia Publishing House, 3558 S. Jefferson Avenue, St. Louis, MO 63118-3968.

This publication may be available in braille, in large print, or on cassette tape for the visually impaired. Please allow 8 to 12 weeks for delivery. Write to Lutheran Blind Mission, 7550 Watson Rd., St. Louis, MO 63119-4409; call toll-free 1-888-215-2455; or visit the Web site: www.blindmission.org.

Manufactured in the United States of America

Table of Contents

Lesson	Title	Bible Story	Page
	Introduction		5
1	**God Does Good Work**	God Creates the World	6
2	**Flesh of My Flesh**	God Creates Adam and Eve	8
3	**Law, Excuses, and Love**	The Fall into Sin	10
4	**I'm So Angry!**	Cain and Abel	12
5	**Saved by the Water**	Noah and the Flood	14
6	**Get Moving**	God Calls Abram	16
7	**Tested to the Limit!**	Abraham and Isaac	18
8	**What Does God Have for You?**	Isaac and Rebekah	20
9	**The Right Light**	Jacob and Esau	22
10	**Betrayed and Befriended**	Joseph	24
11	**Repentance and Forgiveness**	Joseph and His Brothers	26
12	**Having the Time of Your Life**	The Life of Moses	28
13	**A Passover for Our Plagues**	The Ten Plagues	30
14	**God Finds a Way**	Crossing the Red Sea	32
15	**God Gives Bread from Heaven**	Manna in the Wilderness	34
16	**Remember When**	The Bronze Serpent	36
17	**The Walls of Jericho**	The Battle of Jericho	38
18	**A Tough Life**	Ruth	40
19	**My Life Is in Chaos**	Birth of Samuel	42
20	**This Call's for You**	God Calls Samuel	44
21	**Choosing the Right Tool**	David Is Anointed	46
22	**Things Are Getting Difficult**	David and Goliath	48

23	**Kindness from the King**	David and Mephibosheth	50
24	**Giving Our Best**	Solomon Builds the Temple	52
25	**God's Plans and Purposes**	Elijah and the Widow	54
26	**Too Proud?**	Naaman Healed	56
27	**A Curse for Us**	Joash	58
28	**Dealing with Doubt**	Hezekiah	60
29	**For Such a Time as This**	Esther	62
30	**Wholly Forgiven?**	God Calls Isaiah	64
31	**The Greatest Power**	Three Men in the Fiery Furnace	66
32	**A Love for All**	Jonah	68
33	**The Plan**	The Birth of John Foretold	70
34	**Puzzled**	The Birth of Jesus Foretold	72
35	**The Right Time**	The Birth of John	74
36	**The Same Old Story**	The Birth of Jesus	76
37	**The Search Is On**	Boy Jesus in the Temple	78
38	**Blessings of Baptism**	The Baptism of Jesus	80
39	**Beyond Miracles**	The Wedding at Cana	82
40	**You Have the Right Not to Remain Silent**	Jesus Calls His Disciples	84
41	**Which Is Easier?**	Jesus Heals a Paralytic	86
42	**Jesus, My Light**	Jesus Heals a Man Born Blind	88
43	**You're in Good Company!**	Jesus Rejected at Nazareth	90
44	**A Familiar Voice**	Jesus, Our Good Shepherd	92
45	**Resting in Jesus**	Mary and Martha	94
46	**Strengthened by His Glory**	The Transfiguration	96
47	**Fellowship with the Lamb**	The Lord's Supper	98
48	**Godforsaken?!**	Jesus Dies and Is Buried	100
49	**Something Worth Searching For**	The Resurrection of Jesus	102
50	**Can You Believe It?**	Jesus Appears to Thomas	104
51	**Mission Possible**	Jesus Ascends into Heaven	106
52	**What Did You Say?**	God Sends the Holy Spirit	108

Introduction

Junior high students live in a confusing and increasingly complicated world. Their lives are often conflicted and torn as a result of sin. Sometimes it is sin from within, expressing itself in actions and attitudes that run counter to God's Law. Sometimes it is sin from other sources—the actions and attitudes of others—that disrupts their lives. They need God's help to live in the joy and fullness that Christ desires.

Since it is the Gospel that brings spiritual life in Christ to people, it is our goal in these Bible studies for junior high students to connect the Gospel to their life situations. These studies were prepared with four goals in mind. The lessons reflect these goals in the following ways:

1. Each lesson presents the Gospel in ways that will help young people grow in their relationship with Christ.

2. Each lesson is simple and direct—one page of instructions and helps for the Bible study leader and one reproducible page for the students to follow.

3. Each study is practical and easy to prepare. Interaction, variety, and active learning are stressed without requiring excessive preparation by the Bible study leader.

4. Each study deals with the Bible text and seeks to help young people apply the lesson to their lives as they seek to live in Christ.

This book contains fifty-two studies. They can be selected according to the needs of the students and leader and taught in any order.

HELPS FOR PREPARATION AND TEACHING

For ease of use, the leader page and student page for each study are printed side by side in this book, leader's material on the left and the corresponding student page on the right. The appropriate student page should be copied in a quantity sufficient for the class and distributed at the time indicated in the leader's notes.

It is assumed that the Bible class leader will have the usual basic classroom equipment and supplies available—pencils or pens for each student, blank paper (and occasionally tape or marking pens), and a chalkboard or its equivalent (white board, overhead transparency projector, or newsprint pad and easel) with corresponding chalk or markers. Encourage the students to bring their own Bibles so that they can mark useful passages and make personal notes to guide their Bible study between classes. Do provide additional Bibles, however, for visitors or students who do not bring one.

The studies are outlined completely in the leader's notes, including a suggested amount of time for each section of the study. The suggested times will total fifty to fifty-five minutes, the maximum amount most Sunday morning Bible classes have available. Each session begins with an opening activity that may or may not be indicated on the student page. Teachers who regularly begin with prayer should include it before the opening activity. Most other parts of the study, except the closing prayer, are on both the leader page and student page.

An average class size of ten students is assumed. To facilitate discussion, especially when your class is larger than average, it is recommended that you conduct much of the discussion in smaller breakout groups—pairs, triads, or groups of five or six. Instructions to that effect are often included in the guide. If your class is small, you are blessed to already have a "breakout group" and can ignore these suggestions. Leaders who prefer to do all discussion with the class as a whole are also free to ignore breakout-group suggestions.

Most of the studies include one or two "Lesson Extenders" suggestions. Use these when the study progresses more quickly than expected, when your normal session exceeds fifty to fifty-five minutes, or when a suggested activity doesn't work with your group. They can also be used as "during the week" activities.

Of course, the leader is encouraged to review the study thoroughly, well in advance of its presentation. That way the materials can be tailored to your individual students' needs and preferences as well as your own. A prepared and confident teacher normally has better classroom control, which results in a more positive experience for both students and leader.

1. GOD DOES GOOD WORK

Genesis 1:1–2:3

Lesson Focus

Students will explore the wonders of creation and celebrate what God has made as well as His continued care for His creation.

OPENING (2 minutes)

Invite the students to pray with you an ancient prayer in the words of Psalm 145:13–16.

DISCOVERY ZONE (15 minutes)

Distribute copies of the student page and challenge students to consider what they know about the universe God created by thinking about microscopic discoveries and discoveries in space. Invite the students to work together in small groups of three to five to generate the two lists on the student page. You may have to give them some examples to get started—DNA or bacteria; galaxies or black holes. After groups have worked for about five minutes, ask each group to share its list. Remind students that these discoveries were made within the last four hundred years—after the creation of the telescope and the microscope in the seventeenth century. Ask, "How were the people who lived before these discoveries different from you? How is God different before and after these discoveries?" (People's knowledge and lives were changed dramatically by scientific discovery. God, however, is unchanging—constant in His love for us.)

INTO THE WORD (15 minutes)

Invite the students to open their Bibles to Genesis 1. Tell them this is the account of the creation of the entire universe summed up in thirty-one verses. Ask different students to read each of the days of creation.

Instruct the students to turn to section 2 and discuss and respond to each of the selected passages. Some students will not be able to resist questions about life on other planets and the real age of the earth. Allow them to ask the questions without engaging in a debate. You can summarize the discussion in the following manner:

"I don't think we have discovered everything there is to know about the universe. And some of the discoveries of the past seem to contradict each other (like Newtonian physics and quantum physics). One thing has not changed over the centuries—the account of Genesis. The first verse of the Bible is all-encompassing. It is able to give an account of the magnificent and complex creation with simple and even poetic terms. Genesis 1–2 is inclusive of all the scientific discoveries ever made and yet to be made. All of it is good because God made it."

SCIENTIFIC DISCOVERY AND GOD'S GOOD WORK (5 minutes)

Instruct the students to look at the quotes in this section of the student page. Discuss the changing view of the universe in the last few centuries. Despite all the changes in how we see the world, God's view of us has not changed. Nothing is so small (microscopic) or so large (telescopic) that it escaped the creative, protective hand of God. How much more amazing, then, that He puts you and me—our physical and spiritual well-being—above everything else He has created! Heaven and earth will pass away, but because He sent His Son, Jesus, we can spend eternity with Him. Ask the students to write in the space provided on the handout how they would like to be quoted regarding their view of the universe.

CLOSING (3 minutes)

Close the session by listening to the students' quotes on the universe. Read Psalm 121.

LESSON EXTENDERS

✝ Talk about God's continuing care for His creation. You may want to review this section from the explanation of Luther's Small Catechism (Questions 108–111).

God Does Good Work

DISCOVERY ZONE
List discoveries you have heard about that are in the microscopic world and discoveries you have heard about that are in outer space.

....

....

....

Things Too Small to See

....

....

....

Things Far-Off

....

....

....

INTO THE WORD
How does the biblical account of the creation include the discoveries listed in section 1?
Genesis 1:1

....

....

....

Genesis 1:31

....

....

....

Genesis 2:1

....

....

....

SCIENTIFIC DISCOVERY AND GOD'S GOOD WORK

For centuries scientists viewed the universe according to Newtonian physics.
The universe is like a giant machine set in a framework of absolute time and space. Complicated movement can be understood as simple movement of the machine's inner parts, even if these parts can't be visualized. (The view of Sir Isaac Newton, eighteenth century)

With the discovery of quantum physics, scientists reach for new metaphors.
The universe begins to look more like a great thought than like a great machine. (James Jeans, 1930)

[The universe is] a vast porridge of being where nothing is fixed or measurable . . . somewhat ghostly and just beyond our grasp. (Danah Zohar, 1990)

Here is a quote that has endured over many, many centuries.
In the beginning God created the heavens and the earth. . . . God saw all that He had made, and it was very good. (Genesis 1:1, 31)

How would you want to be quoted regarding *your* view of the universe?

....

....

© 2008 Concordia Publishing House. Okay to copy.

2. FLESH OF MY FLESH

Genesis 1:26–2:25

Lesson Focus

Humankind once shared an intimacy with the Creator that was lost as the result of sin. Through the redemptive work of Christ, that intimacy will be restored again in heaven for all believers.

GETTING TO KNOW YOU (10 minutes)

Have students select a partner to work with for this activity. Tell students to spend a few minutes talking with their partner, getting to know that person better. Then have partners sit down back-to-back, and distribute a copy of the student page to each person. Ask students to answer the questions in this section about their partner *without* talking to them. After pairs have had a chance to work, check and see how well they "knew" their partner. Getting to know each other involves spending time together. When we spend time with someone, we begin to develop a level of trust and intimacy with that individual.

UP CLOSE AND PERSONAL (15 minutes)

Chapter 2 of Genesis uses picture language to emphasize the importance of connectedness in all of creation. Ask youth to work together with their partner and watch for signs or images of intimacy or closeness as they read Genesis 1:26–2:25.

God and man—God is described as literally forming and breathing the very life into the man (v. 7).

Humankind and creation—man is to care for earth; man's life depends upon obtaining food from earth (vv. 15–16); man's work or very life involves working the earth (v. 15); man names all the animals (vv. 19–20).

Man and woman—man is lonely (v. 18); the woman is so close to the man that they are bone of bones (vv. 20–21); man and woman are described as becoming one flesh (v. 24).

An image is created for the reader that everything works together for the life of all. There is order, completeness, and togetherness.

You may wish to review Questions 101–7 in the explanation of Luther's Small Catechism with students for more details concerning the connection between the creation and the Creator at the beginning of the world.

PERSONAL CONFLICT (15 minutes)

In the middle of all of these pictures of intimacy are verses 16 and 17, the setting of limits. These are the verses that set up the events in Genesis 3. There is a warning of death here. Even if Adam and Eve did not have their hearts stop the instant they ate of the fruit of the tree in the middle of the garden (Genesis 3:6), something did die. The intimacy, closeness, and interconnectedness of creation died at that very moment. But God's love did not die. That's the Gospel, or Good News!

Have students read Romans 8:18–25. The creation is out of balance. These verses remind us that even creation awaits the second coming of the Lord and the creation of the new heaven and earth. There the believers will live again in an eternal intimate relationship with their Lord and His creation. (See this fulfilled in Matthew 1:1–17.)

CLOSING (5 minutes)

Close with prayer, thanking God for His continuing care of us and all of His creation. Include any special petitions for prayer that may have been suggested by students.

Flesh of My Flesh

GETTING TO KNOW YOU

What color socks is your partner wearing?

What color are your partner's eyes?

Where was your partner born?

What is your partner's favorite candy bar?

If given a ticket to travel anywhere, where would your partner go?

What date was your partner baptized? confirmed?

UP CLOSE AND PERSONAL

Read **Genesis 1:26–2:25**, and list images or pictures that indicate the intimacy between each of the following:

God and man

Humankind and creation

Man and woman (humans and other humans)

PERSONAL CONFLICT

In **verses 16–17**, there is a warning of a death. What would die if the humans went beyond their limits?

Read **Romans 8:18–25**.

What are some of the signs of the frustration of creation today?

What are some of the present sufferings?

What do these verses tell us about our future intimacy with God and His new creation?

© 2008 Concordia Publishing House. Okay to copy.

STUDENT PAGE 2

3. Law, Excuses, and Love

Genesis 3;
John 3:16

Lesson Focus

Our sinful nature tries to make excuses for, or blame others for, our sinful actions. Christ's work on the cross sets us free from sin and blame.

OPENING (5 minutes)

Ask students to imagine this situation. "Your parents just caught you breaking curfew for the third night in a row. You know the consequences, so you try to convince your parents it wasn't your fault. What excuses do you use to beg for leniency?" After a few minutes of discussion, take a poll of your students to determine how many have tried to make excuses for their behavior in order to avoid negative consequences.

IS THAT REALLY WHAT HE SAID? (15 minutes)

Distribute copies of the student page. Have the students read Genesis 2:16–17 and 3:1–5. In small groups, have students answer the questions in this section. Challenge the students to determine what Satan is doing as he seeks to get Adam and Eve to sin. Invite volunteers to share responses, ensuring the group realizes that Satan was seeking to make Adam and Eve doubt the words and intent of God. Ask a volunteer to read Hebrews 10:15–16 and Romans 2:14–15. As the students answer the question, help them understand that every person has a conscience as the result of God writing His Law on that person's heart. Help students understand that no one can claim to be ignorant of the difference between right and wrong. But the Law only condemns us; it is Christ who sets us free through His work on Calvary.

SO WHAT'S YOUR EXCUSE? (10 minutes)

God has written His Law on the hearts of all people. No one has a credible excuse for not knowing the Law. Let's see what happened to Adam and Eve as a result of giving in to Satan's temptation. Ask a volunteer to read Genesis 3:6–13. In discussing the questions, help students understand that, just as Adam and Eve faced consequences, we, too, face consequences when we sin. Despite having no credible excuse for our sinful actions, we try to escape the consequences by blaming God, Satan, and others as well.

IS THAT REALLY WHAT HE DID? (15 minutes)

Ask volunteers to read Genesis 3:14–24; John 3:16; and Psalm 33:20–22. In drawing students' attention to Genesis 3:15, help them understand that God is telling the serpent that the offspring of the woman, Jesus, will crush the head of the serpent, Satan. He is also saying Satan will bruise the heel of Jesus. This is the first Gospel declaration in Scripture as God describes the crucifixion of His Son. Help students see that Gospel message repeated in John 3:16 and determine how they can express to others that God's love is forever and for all. Psalm 89:27–29 connects the lineage of David, from which the Savior, Christ, would arise, with God's eternal promise of salvation from sin.

CLOSING (5 minutes)

Close by inviting students to pray in turn, confessing one excuse they have made for a sin and thanking God for giving Jesus so their sins could be forgiven.

Law, Excuses, and Love

IS THAT REALLY WHAT HE SAID?

Read **Genesis 2:16–17** and **3:1–5**.

What specific command did God give Adam and Eve?

....

How did the serpent convince Eve to eat from the forbidden tree?

....

How does Satan get us to break God's laws?

....

How do you know what God's Law says? If you had never heard God's Law, what would tell you the difference between right and wrong?

....

Read **Hebrews 10:15–16** and **Romans 2:14–15**. How do people know God's Law?

....

SO WHAT'S YOUR EXCUSE?

Adam and Eve gave in to the serpent's deceit and ate from the forbidden tree. Adam and Eve faced consequences for their actions. And as still happens today, they tried to escape those consequences.

Read **Genesis 3:6–13**. What consequences did Adam and Eve face as a result of their sin?

....

On whom did Adam and Eve try to blame their sin?

....

In what other instances in Scripture did people try to blame others for their sin?

....

How are our actions similar to those of Adam and Eve?

....

IS THAT REALLY WHAT HE DID?

God loved Adam and Eve and promised them a Savior, despite their sin. And, no matter how many sins we commit or excuses we make, God will never stop loving us.

Read **Genesis 3:14–24**; **John 3:16**; and **Psalm 33:20–22**.

What promise did God make to all people in **Genesis 3:15**?

....

We see that promise fulfilled in the words of **John 3:16**. What response, based on **Psalm 89:27–29**, could you make to those who might say that promise isn't for us today?

....

© 2008 Concordia Publishing House. Okay to copy.

STUDENT PAGE 3

4. I'M SO ANGRY!

Genesis 4:1–16

Lesson Focus

In this lesson, students will explore the things that make them angry. They will be led to see how forgiveness offered through Christ's death and resurrection allows us to put aside anger.

OPENING (10 minutes)

Ask your students, "Whom have you been jealous of? Why were you jealous of that person? What made you want to be like that person or have what they had?"

SIBLING RIVALRY (15 minutes)

Have students read Genesis 4:1–16 out loud. What is the theme of this text? Record their answers. (If envy, anger, or punishment are not offered as answers, suggest these as themes and encourage discussion about them.) Have students work through the questions on the student page. Ask volunteers to share their answers. As you discuss, point out that sin can begin small, but it grows and becomes deadly. Read James 1:14–15, and discuss the progressive steps of sin shown there.

SIN SOLUTION (15 minutes)

Thanks be to God that He sent His Son to rescue us from sin and its results. Have groups of students read the provided Scripture passages and discuss what each one says about sin and God's forgiveness.

Psalm 1:1–3

Proverbs 28:13–14

Isaiah 43:25

Luke 5:20–24

1 John 1:8–9

Allow volunteers to share their group's discoveries. Then invite volunteers to suggest ways we can respond in our lives of faith, especially in situations that threaten to make us angry.

CLOSING (5 minutes)

Close with prayer, asking the Lord to forgive sins, both remembered and forgotten. Ask for strength to resist temptation and forgive those who anger us.

LESSON EXTENDERS

✝ Not all anger is sinful. Anger can be driven by righteousness. Have students review the story of Jesus clearing the temple in John 2:13–17.

I'M SO ANGRY!

SIBLING RIVALRY

Think about someone who makes you angry. What is it about that person that makes you angry?

....

....

Read **Genesis 4:1–16**.

Why was Cain angry with Abel?

....

Why was God angry with Cain?

....

In what ways are we like Cain?

....

....

There were consequences for Cain's sin. What were they? What are the consequences for our sin?

....

....

....

SIN SOLUTION

Psalm 1:1–3

....

Proverbs 28:13–14

....

Isaiah 43:25

....

Luke 5:20–24

....

1 John 1:8–9

....

5. Saved by the Water

Genesis 6:1–9:17

Lesson Focus

As God saved Noah and his family through the flood, God saves us through the water of our Baptism into Jesus Christ!

WATER: DESTROYER OR RESCUER? (10 minutes)

Distribute copies of the student page. Have students jot down five *bad* things and five *good* things about water. Create a master list on the board or newsprint. "Bad" things may include drowning, floodwater destroying property, rotting wood, rusting metal, and breeding ground for mosquitoes. "Good" things could include drinking, growing crops, fighting fires, cleaning, and recreation. Say, "Water can kill and destroy. Water can also rescue and save. God used the water of Noah's flood to preserve humanity in order to save us by the most important water of all—our Baptism!"

HOW WATER SAVED NOAH (20 minutes)

Invite students to respond to the three questions at the beginning of this section. Make sure that students understand these points:

All humans are evil due to our sinful nature (Romans 7:13–25).

God does not treat us in ways we deserve but according to His undeserved mercy in Christ (called grace—Titus 3:4–7).

The most important thing God wants from us is faith—to trust in Jesus alone for the forgiveness of our sins. God provides that gift of faith through the work of His Holy Spirit.

Allow students to work together in breakout groups to read the Bible passages and discuss the questions. Suggested answer: The unbelievers led the believers away from God. This grieved the Lord. The Lord decided to "wipe mankind . . . from the face of the earth" (Genesis 6:7). God gave Noah the faith by which he trusted and obeyed the Lord. The floodwaters destroyed these wicked humans. Noah "built an altar to the Lord" (Genesis 8:20). We also need to hear God's Word regularly and receive the Lord's Supper for forgiveness and the strengthening of our faith. The water that saves us today comes to us in "the washing of rebirth and renewal by the Holy Spirit" of our Baptism (Titus 3:5).

IN CHRIST, WE HAVE ALL BEEN SAVED BY THE WATER! (15 minutes)

Direct students to read the paragraph on the student page and respond to the question. God saved Noah through the flood. He also gave us faith in His Son, Jesus. Through His precious blood, we have been saved through the *flood* of our Baptism! Those "outside the ark" today are all who do not believe in Jesus as their Savior. We can help our friends and others come into the "ark" of Christ's Church through a simple invitation to worship with us!

CLOSING (5 minutes)

Invite the students to think about ways they can "invite others into the ark" of Christ's Church. Then, let them pray individually, in pairs, or in groups using this model: "Lord Jesus, thank You for rescuing me through the water of my Baptism. Use me to invite _____ to worship with me next week. In Your name I pray. Amen."

Saved by the Water

WATER: DESTROYER OR RESCUER?

Jot down five *bad* things and five *good* things about water.

....

....

....

....

....

....

....

....

....

....

HOW WATER SAVED NOAH

Are humans basically *good* or *evil*?

....

Does God treat us in ways we deserve?

....

How does God continue to save and keep us—what means does He use?

....

Read **Genesis 6:1–6**.
What problem happened when believers married unbelievers (**vv. 2–3, 5**)?

....

Read **Genesis 6:7**.
How did God decide to "fix" this problem?

....

Read **Genesis 6:8–7:5**.
How was God's grace displayed in Noah's life?

....

Read **Genesis 7:17–8:1**.
How can we say that God saved Noah and his family *through* water?

....

Read **Genesis 8:18–22**.
What did Noah first do when he stepped off the ark?

....

Read **1 Peter 3:18–21**.
How does God use water to save us today?

....

IN CHRIST, WE HAVE ALL BEEN SAVED BY THE WATER!

The Holy Spirit inspired St. Peter to connect the water that saved Noah and his family with the water of our Baptism "that now saves you also" (**1 Peter 3:21**). Our Lord Jesus—the descendant of Shem—obeyed the Ten Commandments perfectly for us. Through His suffering, death on the cross, and resurrection, Jesus removed from us forever the guilt and punishment our sins deserve. We who believe in Jesus and are baptized into His name are saved by the daily washing away of all our sins!

Knowing that we are saved by the water, how can we help others who still remain "outside the ark"?

....

....

....

© 2008 Concordia Publishing House. Okay to copy.

STUDENT PAGE 5

6. GET MOVING

Genesis 12:1–9

Lesson Focus

God desires to guide us as we listen to Him. As we follow His leading, we receive His blessings as well.

OPENING (10 minutes)

Have a world or regional map displayed in the classroom when the students arrive. Ask the students to use pushpins (or sticky notes) and yarn or string to identify where they came from and places they have been. Discuss how they came to be at this place, how they traveled, and who guided them here.

Follow up by asking, "Whom do you ask for directions to get somewhere you haven't been before? How do you know these directions are reliable?" Help students see that the best directions come from those who have experience or knowledge.

ADDRESS UNKNOWN (15 minutes)

We are not the only ones who have traveled without knowing where we were going. Read the story of Abram in Genesis 12:1–9. Have the students complete the questions on the student page. Discuss their answers. Why is it sometimes harder for us to obey God than it was for Abram? (Sin) God led Abram to obey His commands, strengthened Abram through trials, and blessed him in many ways. How has God promised to bless us as we follow Him? Why? (Help the students understand that God's blessings are not offered as an inducement to get us to follow Him. God works faith in our hearts, empowers us by His Spirit to follow Him, and blesses and supports us along the way because He loves us.)

LEAD THE WAY (10 minutes)

God speaks to us today through His Word. Have students read the verses listed on the student page. What do each of these verses tell us about God's leading? Look at Jeremiah 3:14–15. Who are some of the "shepherds" God has put in your life? How can they help us?

Direct students to read James 3:17. Discuss each of the qualities mentioned in the verse as they relate to wisdom (pure, peace-loving, considerate, submissive, full of mercy and good fruit, impartial, and sincere). Have the students remember these traits as they consider the questions concerning selecting a college on the student page.

CLOSING (5 minutes)

God wants us to follow Him. He knows the way and how we should get there. He has provided us His Word, His Holy Spirit, pastors, parents, and others to help in knowing His will. Pray: "Lord God, thank You for all the ways You help me follow You. Help me to not only listen to You but also follow You like Abram did long ago. Amen."

LESSON EXTENDERS

✝ Have students consider ways that they can invite teens who are new to the community to be part of the youth group.

✝ Prepare a "welcome" package for new people in the community or church.

Get Moving

ADDRESS UNKNOWN

Read **Genesis 12:1–9**, and answer the following questions.

How did Abram know it was the Lord talking to him?

....
....
....
....

Why did it take a great deal of faith for Abram to follow God's leading? Where did that faith come from?

....
....
....
....
....

What promises did God make to Abram?

....
....
....
....
....

LEAD THE WAY

What does each of these verses tell us about God's leading?

Psalm 32:8

....

Psalm 143:10

....

Revelation 7:17

....

Jeremiah 3:14

....

Consider the traits listed in **James 3:17** as you ponder these questions concerning choosing a college or university to attend.

Is it a *pure* university?

....

Are its faculty and campus *peaceable*?

....

Are the faculty and people *considerate*?

....

Are the courses and requirements *reasonable*?

....

Can you be full of *mercy* and *good fruit* there?

....

Could you be *impartial* and *sincere* when you attend there?

....

© 2008 Concordia Publishing House. Okay to copy.

STUDENT PAGE 6

7. Tested to the Limit!

Genesis 22:1–19

Lesson Focus

Young people find their values and beliefs tested daily. This session reveals that faith in Jesus Christ gives God's people the ability to endure those times of testing

OPENING (5 minutes)

As students arrive, see who can hold their breath the longest. Time each person. Talk about how to improve on this skill. Ask if there is a limit to how long people can hold their breath.

HOW FAR WOULD YOU GO? (10 minutes)

Distribute copies of the student page. Every person has limits for behavior. Your students just won't do certain things! Explore some of those limits. Direct the students to the statements on the student page. Ask them to place an **X** in the column that best defines their limit for each issue. Give students time to respond. Discuss their choices.

Then ask, "Have your limits on these issues always stayed the same? Which have changed? Why? Which might change in the future? Why? Are you ever tempted to go past your limit in these or other areas? Explain."

TO THE MOUNTAINTOP! (10 minutes)

Introduce the Bible study: "Abraham was a very important person in the history of our salvation. And yet God tested his faith. Today we explore Genesis 22 to learn more."

Read Genesis 22:1–19, and discuss the questions on the student page with the class. (Human sacrifice was not uncommon in early Old Testament times. Isaac had been promised by God and was special to God's plan for His people. The ram foreshadowed Jesus. Jesus died for us on the cross. In both cases, God acted in love and grace for His people!)

TEST PREPARATION (10 minutes)

Discuss preparations for times of testing. Point out that it is important to get ready for tests. The students may soon be tested with issues like those discussed earlier. How does one face times of testing?

Have the students read Hebrews 11:17–19 and answer the questions from the student page. Discuss their answers.

Have the students read James 1:12 and share their answers to the questions.

CLOSING (10 minutes)

Ask students to complete the "To Think About" statement. After students are finished, close with a group prayer that allows each person to ask God to help with one issue.

LESSON EXTENDERS

✝ Ask students to compare Jesus' suffering and death with Isaac's experience when the ram was substituted as a sacrifice. How are God's love and grace shown?

✝ Talk with students further about making God-pleasing decisions. Pray with them personally. Follow up one-on-one.

Tested to the Limit!

HOW FAR WOULD YOU GO?

Place an **X** in the column that best defines your limit on the issue.

	LIKELY TO DO	MIGHT CONSIDER	NO WAY!
Yell at my parents			
Lie to protect a friend			
Cheat on a test			
Experiment with drugs or alcohol			
Engage in sex before marriage			
Skip school			
Go to an R-rated movie without telling my parents			
Shoot a person			
Keep $20 found near the grocery checkout			
Sell drugs			

TEST PREPARATION

Read **Hebrews 11:17–19**. What was Abraham's source of strength?

How can faith help you handle tests in life?

Read **James 1:12**.
Who are the "blessed"?

How are they "blessed"?

To Think About: The issues where my limits are being tested right now and where I need God's help are . . .

TO THE MOUNTAINTOP! Read **Genesis 22:1–19**.

How did God test Abraham?

Why do you think God asked this sacrifice of Abraham? Was it an unusual request?

What is significant about the way that God resolved the situation?

How did God provide for your sacrifice for sin?

8. WHAT DOES GOD HAVE FOR YOU?

Genesis 24

Lesson Focus

God has awesome plans for us. He provided all we need for salvation through Jesus' sacrifice on the cross. We can trust in Him for all our earthly needs now and in our future.

ROCK-PAPER-SCISSORS (10 minutes)

Before class, draw up a tournament bracket sheet and have students compete in a Rock-Paper-Scissors Tournament. When the winner is determined, discuss the following: How did it feel to compete in this tournament? (Answers will vary.) What is a key to winning? (Good guessing, "luck," chance) How does this reflect how some people (maybe us) plan for the future? (Leaving things to chance, not going to God) Too often, people think that life is nothing but a large game of chance in which you have a good or bad life according to "luck." Through Christ we have definite plans for our future, both in this present time and through all eternity.

DIGGING IN (20 minutes)

Distribute copies of the student page. Read together Genesis 24:1–67. If you have time, have volunteers act out the story as a drama. If time is short, skip verses 39–51 as these retell the story. Discuss how the characters in this story demonstrate their reliance on God's plan for the future: Abraham trusted God to provide a wife for Isaac. The servant trusted that God would lead him to the right girl. Rebekah trusted God and left her family to go to a husband she had never met. Isaac trusted God and married a girl he had never met before.

DIGGING DEEPER (10 minutes)

Allow time for students to answer the questions in this section in pairs or triads. Discuss their insights with the whole group. Abraham wanted a non-Canaanite wife for Isaac. He trusted that God would provide a wife. This was an important aspect of Isaac's future since the Messiah would come from his descendants. God demonstrated His power by providing the servant exactly what he was looking for in Rebekah. God provides a perfect future for us as Christians through Jesus' life, death, and resurrection. Through faith we are made perfect in God's sight, and we will live eternally with God in the perfection of heaven.

TAKING IT HOME (10 minutes)

Encourage students to share areas where they have questions about the plans God has for their future. As Christians, we can trust God for our future and seek His direction for our lives through wise counsel and the study of the Scriptures. God strengthens our faith and trust in Him through participation in the Sacraments and the study of His Word.

CLOSING (2 minutes)

Close with prayer: "Our great Creator, You are the giver of all things good and perfect. It is by Your great love and generosity that we are even able to come to You in prayer. Help us to see the incredible gifts in our life from You, that we may be able to fully experience the great plans You have in store for us. It is in the name of Your greatest gift to us, Jesus, that we pray. Amen."

LESSON EXTENDERS

✝ As we look at how God has provided and is providing, we can have a greater trust to go to Him with all our decisions and plans. Review Psalm 139 with students.

WHAT DOES GOD HAVE FOR YOU?

DIGGING IN
Read together **Genesis 24:1–67**.

In this story, how did these characters demonstrate their reliance on God for future plans?

....

Abraham

....

The servant

....

Rebekah

....

Isaac

....

DIGGING DEEPER
How do we know that Abraham wanted to follow God's plans for the future?

....

What was important about the future of Isaac, Abraham's son?

....

How did God demonstrate His power of providing in this story?

....

How has God provided a perfect future for us as Christians?

....

....

TAKING IT HOME
In what areas of your life do you need God's plans to be shown to you? Write them below.

....

....

....

....

....

Now for each of those areas, how might God reveal His plans to you?

....

....

....

....

For each of those areas, how can you seek God's plans? See **Psalm 20:4–6**; **Proverbs 15:22**; and **Jeremiah 29:11–13**.

....

....

....

....

© 2008 Concordia Publishing House. Okay to copy.

STUDENT PAGE 8

9. THE RIGHT LIGHT

Genesis 25:19–34; 27:1–29

Lesson Focus

Our sinful nature will always choose instant gratification without regard for long-term cost or consequences. As Jesus lives in us through Word and Sacrament, we are able to make choices that are guided by spiritual concerns.

OPENING (5 minutes)

Create a poster announcing a contest. The winner can choose to receive $1,000 instantly or $100 a month for a year. Ask which prize the students would choose. Why did they make that choice?

THINKING ABOUT LIGHT (15 minutes)

Distribute copies of the student page. Give the students five minutes to list the positives and negatives of buying a $100 car.

Invite volunteers to share their responses, and write them on the board or newsprint. Remind students of the hidden costs like insurance, maintenance, and gasoline. Help the students see that a cheap car will have good and bad consequences.

Have the students consider who might be affected by the decision to buy the car. How will this affect their uncle, parents, friends, and siblings? Help the students explore how their decisions have long-term effects on others.

SEEING THE LIGHT (20 minutes)

This section focuses on the choices Esau (Genesis 25:27–34) and Jacob (Genesis 27:1–29) made and God's grace toward them despite bad choices. Have the students read Genesis 25:27–34 aloud. Read and discuss the questions on the student page. Then ask how God helps us even when we make bad decisions.

Have the students read Genesis 27:1–29 as a drama with parts for Isaac, Rebekah, Jacob, Esau, and a narrator. Discuss the questions on the student page. Also ask what effect this trick might have had on the relationships between Jacob, Isaac, Esau, and Rebekah. How did God bless these people in spite of their sin?

BRINGING THE LIGHT (10 minutes)

We often make choices without thinking of the cost in the future. Ask the students, "When are you more likely to act on impulse rather than with lots of thought?" Discuss the Bible passages and questions on the student page. Assure the students that God is at work in their lives, empowering them to make wise decisions because He loves them.

CLOSING (5 minutes)

Hand out index cards to each student. On each card, have students write a decision they are facing in the next month and a possible solution to it. Encourage them to write two positives and two negatives about this decision. Close with a prayer asking for God's wisdom and help with the decision.

LESSON EXTENDERS

Read 1 Kings 3:1–15 to see how young Solomon faced a time of tough choices. Make a list of what was most important to Solomon. List the blessings the Lord gave him for his long-term thinking.

22

THE RIGHT LIGHT

THINKING ABOUT LIGHT

Your uncle just bought a new car. You would like to buy your uncle's old car for $100. List below the long-term positive and negative consequences of buying this car.

positives	negatives

SEEING THE LIGHT

Read **Genesis 25:27–34**. What was Esau's immediate need? What did Jacob demand in trade?

What was the birthright? (See **Genesis 25:5**.) How might its value compare to that of stew?

Suppose you were Esau. What would you have done when Jacob demanded such a high price for stew?

Read **Genesis 27:1–29**. What did Rebekah want for Jacob? Do you think the success of the plan meant God really approved?

Read **Genesis 27:41–44**. What was the ultimate cost of Jacob's success? Do you think his success was worth it?

BRINGING THE LIGHT

Why do *we* make bad choices, decisions that result in harm to us or others?

Read **Romans 7:21–25** and **1 Peter 2:9**. What hope is there when we feel trapped by our sinful nature in bad choices?

© 2008 Concordia Publishing House. Okay to copy.

10. Betrayed and Befriended

Genesis 37; 39–41

Lesson Focus

Young people experience betrayal in their relationships. In this lesson, students will learn that God befriends us and never will betray us. Through the Spirit, He empowers us to forgive those who betray us.

IF . . . (5 minutes)

Have students suggest a situation where someone might be betrayed. Invite students to role-play the event. Say, "Share a time when you were helped by a friend or a sibling. When you are in trouble, what person do you most often count on? Has this person ever betrayed you?" Distribute copies of the student page. Allow students time to complete the three sentences on the student page. Invite volunteers to share their answers.

I CAN'T BELIEVE THEY DID THIS! (15 minutes)

Assign individuals or groups to summarize the Bible cases of betrayal. Ask, "How might these experiences have changed Joseph? Do you think people generally grow closer to God because of their trials or turn away from Him? Defend your answer."

GOD TO THE RESCUE (10 minutes)

Assign individuals or groups to read the Bible accounts and summarize how God befriended Joseph. Read Romans 8:28 aloud. Say, "God promises to bring good from our troubles, but He does not promise to take all our troubles away. Why not? How was this true for Joseph? How do you suppose Joseph might have been changed because of his troubles?"

I'M THE FORGIVEN BETRAYER (10 minutes)

Have volunteers read the verses aloud. Discuss the questions on the student page. Help students to understand that our salvation does not depend on what we do but on what Jesus did for us when He willingly gave up His life, taking the punishment for our sins.

MY TURN TO FORGIVE (10 minutes)

Have volunteers read the verses aloud. Say, "Why is it so hard to forgive? Our sinful nature always desires to take revenge, so we cannot forgive without God's help. But as the Holy Spirit works faith in our hearts, He transforms us so we become more like Jesus and are able to forgive. When we forgive, it heals us as well as the person who is forgiven."

CLOSING (5 minutes)

Invite students to pray silently for someone who has hurt them and to ask for God's help to forgive. Lead the class in this prayer:

"Dear Jesus, forgive me for the times I have betrayed You, especially when I have not forgiven those who hurt me. Send Your Holy Spirit to transform me so I can be more like You. I pray in Your name, Jesus, knowing You love me unconditionally and answer every prayer. Amen."

LESSON EXTENDERS

✝ Jesus knew ahead of time that He would be betrayed. How did He treat His betrayer (Matthew 26:20–25, 49–50)?

✝ Have students cite biblical examples of people befriending their enemies (see Luke 10:33–35; 23:34, 40–43; Acts 7:59–60).

Betrayed and Befriended

IF . . .
If my brother was jealous of me, he might . . .

....

....

If I was falsely accused of something, my friends would . . .

....

....

If I was betrayed by my family and friends, I would . . .

....

....

I CAN'T BELIEVE THEY DID THIS!
How was Joseph betrayed

by his brothers? (**Genesis 37:12–36**)

....

by his master's wife? (**Genesis 39:7–20**)

....

by his fellow prisoners? (**Genesis 40**)

....

GOD TO THE RESCUE
How did God befriend Joseph in his troubles

while he was a slave? (**Genesis 39:2–6**)

....

while he was a prisoner? (**Genesis 39:21–23**)

....

when he was called before Pharaoh? (**Genesis 41:9–57**)

....

I'M THE FORGIVEN BETRAYER
How have we betrayed God? How does He befriend us?

Romans 6:23

....

....

....

Ephesians 2:1–5

....

....

....

MY TURN TO FORGIVE
How can we befriend those who betray us?

Ephesians 4:32

....

....

....

1 Thessalonians 5:15–18

....

....

....

© 2008 Concordia Publishing House. Okay to copy.

STUDENT PAGE 10

11. Repentance and Forgiveness

Genesis 42–45; 50:15–21

Lesson Focus

The account of Joseph forgiving his brothers demonstrates a model for forgiving those who sin against us and assures the believer of forgiveness in Christ Jesus.

Note to teacher: People often speculate regarding why Joseph didn't immediately tell his brothers who he was. Luther taught that God guided Joseph's actions in order to lead his brothers to repentance for their sins of selling Joseph into slavery and lying to their father. Help students to understand that each of Joseph's actions helped lead his brothers toward confession and repentance.

THE ACT OF FORGIVING (5 minutes)

Distribute copies of the student page, and ask youth to complete this section. Discuss responses and affirm each student.

FIRST INTERACTION (10 minutes)

Ask students to skim the passage. Discuss the events broadly so that students know the story. Ask a volunteer to read Genesis 42:21–22, 28, and 30, and have students consider the questions on the student page as the volunteer reads. Responses: the brothers immediately attribute this bad event to their sin of selling Joseph into slavery; among themselves they blame or attribute the event to God; to their father they blame Joseph (i.e., "the man who is lord over the land"—Genesis 42:30). Since they have not repented and confessed their sin, they cannot be honest with their father.

SECOND INTERACTION (10 minutes)

Again ask students to skim the chapters, and discuss major events. Ask a volunteer to read Genesis 44:12–13, 16, and 30–33 as others listen and consider the questions on the student page. Discuss how the tearing of one's garments may indicate sorrow or repentance; Judah states that God has uncovered their guilt. He is willing to accept punishment as a slave, and he shows compassion toward his father in wanting Benjamin to return home.

THIRD INTERACTION (10 minutes)

Next, direct students to Joseph's response to Judah's repentance. Ask one or two students to read aloud Genesis 45:4–14. Joseph offers forgiveness in several ways: he tells his brothers not to be distressed or angry with themselves, he points to God's hand in all that happened, he expresses a desire to save them and to have them live with him, and he kisses each of them. His faith is seen as he is able to forgive his brothers and as he focuses upon the providence of God.

Review the major events of Genesis 50:1–21. Ask a volunteer to read aloud Genesis 50:15–17 while all students consider the questions. Discuss how the brothers must have confessed their sin to their father and how they are now afraid and doubt Joseph's forgiveness.

Direct students to Joseph's response, and ask students to silently read Genesis 50:19–21. Joseph offers the same reassurance as before—God is in control; don't be afraid; I will care for you.

CLOSING (10 minutes)

Ask students to consider and discuss the following questions: Are you ever slow in repenting and confessing your sins?

How are Joseph's actions an example of how God responds to our sinfulness?

How can Genesis 50:20 comfort you at times when people treat you wrongly?

Close in prayer.

Repentance and Forgiveness

THE ACT OF FORGIVING

Consider the incidents below, and mark how easy or difficult forgiving would be.

	Forgive Easily	Forgive with Difficulty	Not Sure I Could Forgive
A friend spoke unkind words to you.			
Your mom forgot to do something she promised she would do.			
A drunk driver hit your sister, and she became paralyzed.			
What would be something you consider unforgivable?			

FIRST INTERACTION

Read **Genesis 42:6–38** to review the brothers' first interaction in more than twenty years! Consider the following:

How do the brothers reveal that they have guilty consciences for selling Joseph into slavery (**vv. 21–22**)?

How does Joseph offer God's grace and forgiveness to his brothers?

Whom do they blame (**vv. 28 and 30**)?

Why did they change the object of their blame?

Are the brothers repentant?

SECOND INTERACTION

What sign of sorrow and repentance is seen in **Genesis 44:12–13**?

How can **Genesis 44:16, 30–33** be seen as a confession of sin?

THIRD INTERACTION

What does **Genesis 44:15–18** indicate about the brothers' confession of sin?

Read **Genesis 45:4–14**. How does Joseph offer forgiveness to his brothers?

How is Joseph's faith in God expressed?

Read **Genesis 50:20**. How does Joseph offer forgiveness?

Is this "better" than just saying, "You are forgiven"?

How does he view all the events of his life?

© 2008 Concordia Publishing House. Okay to copy.

STUDENT PAGE 11

12. Having the Time of Your Life

Exodus 2–4

Lesson Focus

Many Bible characters were ordinary people that God used for great things. God uses young people today to be leaders in their churches.

HIGHLIGHTS OF YOUR LIFE (15 minutes)

Distribute copies of the student page. Ask students to work alone to complete the first section, entitled "Highlights of Your Life." Students are to choose any five major events in their lives and write them across the top. They can be positive or negative. You may wish to give a brief account of your top five events as an example. Be available to help individual students. Beneath each highlight are spaces to give Life Values scores. For each highlight, have students rate how important (valuable) this event is on a scale of one through ten, with ten being greatest.

When the students have completed the chart, encourage them to share with a partner. Make sure everyone is in a group of two or three. Ask students to note any similarities or differences.

MOSES AND ME (30 minutes)

Working in the same groups, have the students complete the chart for Moses' life. Students should use the Bible references on the chart to review five events in the life of Moses. Remind them that no one knows for sure how Moses felt about these experiences, but they should imagine how he may have felt. Encourage the groups to share what they discover.

What kinds of comparisons can students make between their lives and Moses' life? In spite of Moses' faults, God used him to be the leader of His chosen people. In spite of our sins, God uses us as well. What leadership opportunities does God give young people today?

CLOSING (5 minutes)

Dear God, You are the Great "I AM." You were there for Abraham and Moses. You rescued Your people from slavery and, in Jesus Christ, You saved the whole world from sin. We are grateful that we can call upon You for help and deliverance from our slavery to sin. In the name of Jesus we pray. Amen.

LESSON EXTENDERS

✝ Ask the students if they know why their parents gave them their name. Does it have special meaning? How did Moses get his name? What did it mean? (See Exodus 2:10.) What name was Moses to give to the God of all gods? (See Exodus 3:14.) What a wonderful privilege to be able to address our God and Savior by His name. He did not remain unknown and unavailable. We can come to Him in prayer, call upon His name, and pray in the name of His Son, Jesus.

Having the Time of Your Life

HIGHLIGHTS OF YOUR LIFE—MEMORABLE EVENTS

LIFE VALUES					
SECURITY (A sense of protection and well-being)					
WEALTH (What you need for a good living)					
JOY (A sense of deep happiness)					
SPIRITUALITY (A close relationship with God)					
FRIENDSHIP (Supportive and caring friends)					

MOSES AND ME—MOSES' LIFE EVENTS

LIFE VALUES	Exodus 1:8–14, 22; 2:1–10	Exodus 2:11–15	Exodus 2:15–22	Exodus 2:23–3:17	Exodus 3:18–20, 4:27–31
SECURITY (A sense of protection and well-being)					
WEALTH (What you need for a good living)					
JOY (A sense of deep happiness)					
SPIRITUALITY (A close relationship with God)					
FRIENDSHIP (Supportive and caring friends)					

© 2008 Concordia Publishing House. Okay to copy.

STUDENT PAGE 12

13. A Passover for Our Plagues

Exodus 5:1–12:30

Lesson Focus

Because of our sin, we are plagued by broken relationships, sickness, and death. Jesus came as our Passover Lamb to rescue us from sin, death, and the devil.

PICK A PEST (5 minutes)

Begin the class time by asking students to talk about an insect that really "bugs" them. Talk about how such little animals can really bother us. Today's lesson will talk about how something that seems to be small can affect us completely.

PICK A PLAGUE (15 minutes)

Distribute copies of the student page. Allow students to work alone or in small groups to research one or more of the plagues from the list on the student page. Students should summarize the plague and how it affected the Egyptians and the Israelites. What was Pharaoh's reaction each time? Emphasize that the plagues were sent by God as consequences for Pharaoh's failure to obey Him.

THE PASSOVER (10 minutes)

Allow students to work together in small groups to study the first Passover as described in Exodus 12:1–30. Give students time to answer the questions found on the student page. When you sense that students have completed the questions, allow volunteers to share their insights.

PERSONAL PLAGUE (10 minutes)

Assign volunteers to read aloud each of the passages listed on the student page. Discuss the "personal plague" that each of us suffers from. We each inherit and express our sinful condition. We are sinful from our very birth (original sin). In addition we daily sin against the Law of God (actual sin).

THE PASSOVER LAMB (10 minutes)

Have student volunteers read aloud the verses from the student page. Lead students in a discussion concerning the role of Christ as our Passover Lamb. Help students to understand the important connection between the first Passover and the work of Christ on our behalf through His suffering, death, and resurrection. For the first Passover, the blood of an unblemished lamb was used to mark the homes of the Israelites for the plague to "pass over" those households. Jesus, the unblemished, sinless Lamb of God shed His blood on the cross in order that we may "pass over" into eternal life with Him.

PRAISE PRAYER (5 minutes)

Close by asking students to share specific prayer requests. Lead the class in a prayer of thanks for Christ's sacrifice so that we may gain eternal life. Allow students to speak their petitions, or you may pray about their requests.

LESSON EXTENDERS

✝ Jesus is our Prophet, Priest, and King. Use Questions 125 and 148 in *Luther's Small Catechism with Explanation* to review these roles of Jesus. How does each of these roles fit with the Passover?

A Passover for Our Plagues

PICK A PLAGUE

Select one of the plagues on Egypt and read the verses listed. How did that plague affect the Egyptians? the Israelites? What was the purpose for the plagues? What was Pharaoh's reaction?

Blood—**Exodus 7:14–24**

Frogs—**Exodus 8:1–15**

Gnats—**Exodus 8:16–19**

Flies—**Exodus 8:20–31**

Livestock—**Exodus 9:1–7**

Boils—**Exodus 9:8–12**

Hail—**Exodus 9:13–35**

Locusts—**Exodus 10:1–20**

Darkness—**Exodus 10:21–29**

Firstborn—**Exodus 11:1–10; 12:29–30**

THE PASSOVER

Read **Exodus 12:1–28**.

What preparations were the Israelites supposed to make for the Passover?

What marking caused the Lord to pass by?

The celebration of Passover contains significance for us as Christians. What is the connection? (See **Luke 22:7–20**.)

PERSONAL PLAGUE

Romans 3:9–1; 19–20; Ephesians 2:1

What do all of these verses tell us about our condition before God?

How did we get this way?

THE PASSOVER LAMB

John 1:29; Romans 5:15–19; 1 Corinthians 15:54–57

In what way is Jesus our (your) Passover Lamb?

© 2008 Concordia Publishing House. Okay to copy.

STUDENT PAGE 13

14. GOD FINDS A WAY

Exodus 12:31–42; 13:17–15:21

Lesson Focus

God rescues the Israelites by miraculously parting the Red Sea and allowing them to walk through the sea on dry ground. Similarly, God makes a way for us, providing salvation and eternal life through the death and resurrection of Jesus Christ.

GOD, I'M STUCK! (5 minutes)

Encourage student discussion about times in their lives when they've felt "stuck"—perhaps they've faced a difficult family issue, a move was upsetting, or they have struggled with academic issues.

LORD, PLEASE HELP! (15 minutes)

Hand out copies of the student page. Have students work in groups to skim Exodus 13:17–15:21 (if time is short, read Exodus 14:13–31). Identify the main events of this narrative. The Israelites are afraid, so Moses reassures them (14:13–14); Moses obeys God's command to part the waters (14:15–22); the Egyptians follow (14:23–25); the Egyptians are destroyed (14:26–28); and Israel is saved (14:29–31).

STAND FIRM! (20 minutes)

Have students read 2 Chronicles 20:17; 1 Samuel 12:16, 22; Deuteronomy 1:29–30; and Psalm 46:10. Discuss the promises of God found in these verses (possibilities include: the Lord will be with you; the Lord will fight for you; see the salvation of God).

From 2 Corinthians 1:18–22, students learn that for the Christian the promises of God are always fulfilled in Christ. In Him we stand firm, trusting in His kindness and mercy, which He showed by dying on the cross for our sins.

GOOD NEWS HEADLINES (10 minutes)

Allow students to write two newspaper headlines—one about the Israelites' miraculous escape from Pharaoh and one about God working in their own lives. Examples might be "God's Chosen People Saved from Disaster" and "Corey Saved from Sins through Baptism," or "God Works Miracle at Red Sea" and "God Works Miracle in Corey's Life!"

CLOSING (5 minutes)

Read again Exodus 14:13–14 to the students. Then close with prayer: "Dear Father in heaven, we thank You for the salvation You have given us through the death of Your Son on the cross. This salvation we see with eyes of faith. Thank You for not leaving us alone in our problems and difficulties. Through Your Word You show us a path through our problems that will lead us to greater faith in You. Through Jesus, we pray. Amen."

LESSON EXTENDERS

✝ Read Moses' song in Exodus 15:1–18. How does Moses' confidence and joy compare to his earlier attitude when he first encountered God at the burning bush (Exodus 3)?

✝ Read Hebrews 11:23–29. What do these New Testament verses reveal about Moses' changed attitude?

✝ Study the Easter hymn "Come, You Faithful, Raise the Strain" (*LSB* 487; *LW* 141), and discuss how it connects this Old Testament story and Easter.

God Finds a Way

LORD, PLEASE HELP!
Skim **Exodus 13:17–15:21**, and outline the events of this section:

What can you learn from what the Israelites went through on their escape from Egypt?

STAND FIRM!
Read **2 Chronicles 20:17**; **1 Samuel 12:16–22**; **Deuteronomy 1:29–30**; and **Psalm 46:10**. What is the theme repeated in these verses as well as in **Exodus 14:13–14**?

What are some of the promises of God in these verses?

Read **2 Corinthians 1:18–22**. What is the promise concerning Christ in which we trust? In whom do we "stand firm"?

GOOD NEWS HEADLINES
Pretend you are a newspaper reporter writing an article about the Israelites' escape from Egypt. Write a headline about their escape. Then, write a second headline about God's work in your life.

STUDENT PAGE 14

15. God Gives Bread from Heaven

Exodus 16:1–17:7

Lesson Focus

Just as God provided for the Israelites, God provides all we need in body and spirit, especially our need for forgiveness through our Savior, Jesus Christ.

OPENING (5 minutes)

Engage students in a discussion about complaining. Why do people complain? They may be unhappy, uncomfortable, or dissatisfied with life. Ask students how complaining affects a person spiritually. What does it show about a person's faith?

Sometimes complaining reveals a lack of faith. People aren't satisfied with the gifts God has given them. With a partner, have students describe a time when they have been complainers. What kinds of things did they complain about? How might their complaining have affected them spiritually?

GRUMBLING BEFORE THE LORD (15 minutes)

Distribute copies of the student page. Allow students to respond to the question about the attitude of the Israelites. Discuss the magnitude of this miracle, the devastation on their enemies, and the Israelites' complete victory. Then have students read Exodus 16:1–3 and answer the questions on the student page. It may help to review the previous lesson about the Red Sea miracle.

STUBBORN HEARTS (10 minutes)

Have students read Exodus 16:19–30 and answer the questions on the student page. The Israelites' lack of faith seems obvious to us as we read these verses. Why couldn't they just trust in God? They had seen amazing works of God, and yet they still struggled in their faith.

GOD'S BEST GIFTS (15 minutes)

In this section, students discover the parallels between a lack of faith and grumbling. Like the disciples, we need increased faith, and yet we still doubt, complaining about our lives, not trusting that God knows what's best for us. And as He did with the complaining Israelites, God still forgives and loves us in spite of our sin.

Note that the verses in Galatians describe the characteristics of a Christian as fruit of the Spirit. The Holy Spirit stirs up these attitudes/characteristics by increasing our faith. Patience in particular wrestles against complaining. As we remember our Baptism, hear God's Word, and receive the Lord's Supper, our faith in the crucified Christ grows. Just as He fed the Israelites with the bread in the wilderness, God feeds us with the bread of life, His very body, in Holy Communion.

LESSON EXTENDERS

† Read John 6:25–40. How does Jesus describe Himself in these verses? The manna satisfied the Israelites during forty years of wandering in the desert. Our Lord Jesus satisfies our needs for eternity.

God Gives Bread From Heaven

GRUMBLING BEFORE THE LORD

How long do you think the Israelites should have been confident and joyful in their saving God, who led them through the Red Sea?

....

....

Why did the Israelites complain to God (**Exodus 16:1–3**)?

....

....

How did God respond to their grumbling (**Exodus 16:4**)?

....

....

What did God give to the Israelites (**Exodus 16:13–18, 31**)?

....

....

STUBBORN HEARTS

Read **Exodus 16:19–26**. God gave these gifts to the Israelites freely, but what did God demand regarding each day's gathering?

....

Did the Israelites follow these instructions (**Exodus 16:27–30**)?

....

....

....

....

GOD'S BEST GIFTS

Read **Luke 17:5–6**. What do the disciples ask Jesus to do for them?

....

....

Describe how a lack of faith is related to complaining before the Lord, especially as you learned from the story of the Israelites.

....

....

....

Read **Galatians 5:22–24**. What characteristics does the Holy Spirit work in the hearts of Christians? Identify one in particular that relates to grumbling.

....

....

....

Praise God for the gift of faith! Read **Galatians 2:20**. How does this verse reassure you?

....

....

....

....

16. REMEMBER WHEN

Numbers 21:4–9;
Joshua 3–4

Lesson Focus

God's people remember what He has done for them throughout their lives. Memorials and celebrations are designed to help future generations remember God's protection and provision.

MEMORIALS (10 minutes)

Distribute copies of the student page. Have the students describe the meaning and purpose of the United States monuments and answer the questions from this section. Allow time for student discussion.

The students' answers will vary. Obviously these memorials would not have the same meaning for people of other nations. They commemorate events that happened to the United States and affect the lives of its citizens.

Encourage the students to think of war memorials or memorials for local historical events. Even homes and battlefields could be considered. These can bring to mind an important event or person and teach important lessons for the people of today.

A RIVERSIDE MEMORIAL (15 minutes)

Ask students to consider what their memorial to God would look like. After a minute or two of discussion, read the story of Israel crossing the Jordan in Joshua 3–4. Have students work together in small groups to answer the questions from the student page.

Moses is dead, and the Israelites have powerful nations to conquer. One would expect them to be nervous and scared. God parts the Jordan River during flood season so the people can walk across safely. The miracle taught the people that the Lord would conquer all their enemies just as He tamed the river. God commands the Israelites to gather twelve stones from the center of the river and use them to build a memorial. This memorial was to remind them and future generations of the great miracle and covenant of God. The memorial would let all the nations know that God is powerful and should be feared.

SNAKES AND SIN (10 minutes)

Have students read Numbers 21:4–9 and discuss the questions on the student page.

This memorial was built at God's command to remind the people of God's forgiveness and love. God could have destroyed them all but instead provided mercy for those who looked at the memorial and trusted in His mercy. The structure would have reminded them of their sin and the mercy of the very God they had rebelled against. The bronze serpent also serves to remind us of God's promise of forgiveness and salvation.

BUILDING OUR OWN MEMORIAL (15 minutes)

Before class, gather about sixty craft sticks, three 5 x 12-inch sheets of poster board or cardboard, felt-tip pens of different colors, and glue. Tape the three sheets of poster board together into a 12-inch triangular tower. (You may wish to cut another piece of poster board to fit in the triangle at the top of the tower and tape it in place for extra support.)

Remind students that we also have many blessings from God to remember today. We can make a memorial to remember what God has done for us and to witness to others about the power of our God. Hand out craft sticks to students, and ask them to write something on them that God has done for the nation, the community or church, or their family.

Glue the craft sticks onto the tower you have made so that each face is covered with the craft sticks listing blessings from God. Display this tower at church so others can see it and thank God for His blessings.

CLOSING (5 MINUTES)

Invite the students to close with a prayer of thanks to the Lord for one thing on the memorial. You may close by singing or speaking together the common doxology.

REMEMBER WHEN

MEMORIALS
What does each of these United States monuments recall?

Mount Rushmore, South Dakota
....

Lincoln Memorial, Washington DC
....

Washington Monument, Washington DC
....

Vietnam Veterans Memorial, Washington DC
....

The Gateway Arch, St. Louis, Missouri
....

Would these monuments have the same meaning for someone who is not a citizen of the United States? Why or why not?
....
....
....

To whom might the Vietnam Memorial mean the most? Why?
....
....
....

Are there any memorials in your area? What are they meant to help recall?
....
....
....

A RIVERSIDE MEMORIAL
If you were going to build a memorial for God, what would it look like? What would you like your memorial to say about God?
....
....

While waiting to cross the Jordan River and enter the Promised Land, what do you think the people were doing and feeling (Joshua 3:1)?
....
....

What miracle does God perform here (Joshua 3:15–16)? What was the purpose of the miracle (Joshua 3:10–11)?
....
....
....

Having crossed the river, what command does God give the Israelites (Joshua 4:3)? What was the purpose of the memorial (Joshua 4:6–7)?
....
....
....

Of what will the memorial remind all people (Joshua 4:24)?
....
....

SNAKES AND SIN
Look at another "memorial" that God commanded to be made in **Numbers 21:4–9**.

What was built, and what was its purpose (21:8–9)? How did this show God's mercy?
....
....
....

What would the sight of this structure remind the people about themselves?
....

Of what does this memorial remind us?
....
....

STUDENT PAGE 16

17. THE WALLS OF JERICHO

Joshua 5:13–6:27

Lesson Focus

God demonstrates His power over the physical obstacle at Jericho. In the same way, God's power removes the spiritual obstacle of sin in our lives through the death and resurrection of Jesus.

THAT'S IMPOSSIBLE! (10 minutes)

Show a video clip of *Ripley's Believe It or Not* or another video of amazing feats. Or bring in a copy of the *Guinness Book of World Records* and read a few of the more amazing things. Ask, "What was one of the most amazing things you've seen in your life? Have you ever been asked to do something that seemed impossible? What was it?"

OPENING UP SCRIPTURE (10 minutes)

Read together Joshua 5:13–6:27. Allow time for students to work in groups to answer the questions on the student page. Who meets Joshua near Jericho? ("The commander of the army of the Lord"; "the Lord" in 6:2; perhaps even Jesus) What is strange about the statement in Joshua 6:2? (The Lord said the city had been delivered to Joshua, though it was still surrounded by a wall.) What is the plan of attack from God to Joshua? (To march around the city for seven days) What did the men do once the city walls fell down? (They devoted everything to God, destroyed all living things) Who was saved from the city? (Rahab the prostitute and her family) Later in Scripture the faith of Rahab is noted. (See Hebrews 11:31 and James 2:25.)

DIGGING DEEPER (10 minutes)

Discuss the questions from this section as a group. What did Joshua learn when it came to preparing battle plans? (Trust God's plan, He will bring success) How could the Lord tell Joshua that the city was delivered to him? (God knows how all things will work out; He controls everything.) Why was it important to destroy all living things in the city? (God demanded it; it shows how God is completely holy.) How is the saving of Rahab's family a demonstration of God's grace? (Rahab was a prostitute, but God saved her because of her faith [Hebrews 11:31].)

KNOCKING DOWN THE WALL (10 minutes)

Have students read Romans 8:31–39 and work alone to complete this section. Discuss their answers with the whole group. What impossible obstacles, or "walls," are you facing in life? (Answers will vary—school, temptation, family) What battle plan do you think God has for you to overcome these "walls"? (Looking to Him, trusting in His promises) What things in your life do you feel need to be completely destroyed? (Answers will vary; allow students to keep answers private.) How did God tell us that we had victory over these "walls" in our life? (When Jesus died on the cross, He defeated sin, death, and the devil.) How can we know victory when we are looking at a great big wall? (We rely on God's power. We will face troubles and hardship because we live in a sin-tainted world. Yet nothing is greater than what Christ has already defeated on the cross—sin, death, and the devil.) When will we fully experience victory? (When we get to heaven)

CLOSING THOUGHT (5 minutes)

Say, "It's hard to feel like the victor when you face obstacles in life. But we can trust in the promises of God that He has defeated sin, death, and the devil now and for all eternity." Pray together, "Almighty Lord God, You hold all things in the palm of Your hand. Forgive us for doubting Your power and Your Word. Help us to look first to You and then to follow Your plans. Thank You for the deliverance You give us through the life, death, and resurrection of Your Son, Jesus, in whose name we pray. Amen."

THE WALLS OF JERICHO

OPENING UP SCRIPTURE

Read together **Joshua 5:13–6:27**.

Who meets Joshua near Jericho?

....

....

What is strange about the statement in **Joshua 6:2**?

....

....

....

What is the plan of attack from God to Joshua?

....

....

....

What did the men do once the city walls fell down?

....

....

Who was saved from the city?

....

....

....

DIGGING DEEPER

What did Joshua learn when it came to preparing battle plans?

....

How could the Lord tell Joshua that the city was delivered to him?

....

Why was it important to destroy all living things in the city?

....

How is the saving of Rahab's family a demonstration of God's grace?

....

KNOCKING DOWN THE WALL

Read **Romans 8:31–39**. What impossible obstacles, or "walls," are you facing in life?

....

....

What battle plan do you think God has for you to overcome these "walls"?

....

What things in your life do you feel need to be completely destroyed?

....

....

How did God tell us that we had victory over these "walls" in our life?

....

How can we know victory when we are looking at a great big wall?

....

When will we fully experience victory?

....

© 2008 Concordia Publishing House. Okay to copy.

18. A TOUGH LIFE

Ruth 1

Lesson Focus

Just as God provided for Ruth, He provides for us, even in the toughest of times.

OPENING (10 minutes)

Find a video clip that has a character in a series of mishaps or problems in a short amount of time. Possibilities include *The Pink Panther* or *Mr. Bean*. Show a short clip to illustrate someone having a really tough time. If that's not possible, share from your own life a time when things were not going well. Ask, "Who is your favorite character who can never seem to get things right? What are some examples of really tough times you've heard of?"

OPENING THE WORD (15 minutes)

Give students a copy of the student page. Read Ruth 1. Allow them time to answer the questions. Review their answers with the whole group. What things went wrong for Naomi? (Famine, death of her husband, death of her two sons) See verse 6. What prompted Naomi to go back to her people? (She heard that God was providing for them.) Why did Naomi encourage Ruth and Orpah to stay? (To find husbands) What was each woman's response? (Orpah returned to her people; Ruth went on with Naomi.) When they returned home to Bethlehem, why did Naomi want to be called Mara? (*Naomi* means "pleasant," but she felt *Mara,* or "bitter.")

DIGGING DEEPER (15 minutes)

Have students work in pairs to answer the questions. Discuss their findings with the whole group. Ruth was a Moabite woman, and the Moabites were considered immoral by Jewish people. Ruth was also the great-grandmother of King David. How did Ruth demonstrate faithfulness to God in verses 16–17? (She pledged her faithfulness to Him.) How did God demonstrate faithfulness to Naomi? (He allowed her to return home and gave her Ruth.) Why do you think Naomi returned home if she felt that God had brought misfortune on her? (She still trusted God's promises to take care of His people.)

TAKING IT HOME (10 minutes)

Read together 2 Corinthians 1:3–11. Discuss Paul's message of hope and salvation that he shares with the Church at Corinth. Note especially verse 10. From what does God deliver us? (Sin, death, and the devil) Allow time to discuss the rest of the questions in this section. When have you felt like everything was going wrong? (Answers will vary.) Who helped you out and how? When have you felt completely cared for? Who did this and how? Where have you seen examples of God's faithfulness in tough times?

CLOSING THOUGHTS (5 minutes)

Say, "At times we may feel like a *Mara,* or bitter, about our circumstances. The Book of Ruth shows us that even in the toughest times God will provide us with what we need. Ruth took care of Naomi, and Ruth was later taken care of by Boaz, her new husband. In all this we see a picture of God's relationship to us through the redemption, or saving work, of Jesus Christ." Pray, "Heavenly Father, Your work is incredible! You always have a plan for us and our lives. Forgive us for doubting that plan and making up our own plans. We thank You for providing us with all we need, especially for giving us Your Son, our Redeemer and Savior, Jesus Christ. In His name we pray. Amen."

A Tough Life

OPENING THE WORD

Read **Ruth 1**. What things went wrong for Naomi?

See **verse 6**. What prompted Naomi to go back to her people?

Why did Naomi encourage Ruth and Orpah to stay?

What was each woman's response?

When they returned home to Bethlehem, why did Naomi want to be called Mara?

DIGGING DEEPER

Ruth was a Moabite woman, and the Moabites were considered immoral by Jewish people. Ruth was also the great-grandmother of King David. How did Ruth demonstrate faithfulness to God in **verses 16–17**?

How did God demonstrate faithfulness to Naomi?

Why do you think Naomi returned home if she felt that God had brought misfortune on her?

TAKING IT HOME

When have you felt like everything was going wrong?

Who helped you out and how?

When have you felt completely cared for?

Who did this and how?

Where have you seen examples of God's faithfulness in tough times?

© 2008 Concordia Publishing House. Okay to copy.

19. MY LIFE IS IN CHAOS

1 Samuel 1:1–2:11; 3

Lesson Focus

Students will discover that God uses what seems to be chaos in the world in which they live to bring about His plan of salvation. By faith we can depend on His watchful eye to help us through any situation as He delivers us from Satan.

CHAOTIC LIVES (15 minutes)

Distribute copies of the student page. Allow students to work together to complete the questions concerning their schedules and lives. Allow groups to share some of the chaos that they may be facing in their lives. Open with a prayer asking God to allow us to slow down and hear His Word for us this day.

THE UPS AND DOWNS OF LIFE (15 minutes)

Hannah certainly felt like her life was in chaos, especially when the most important value to a Hebrew female at that time was to have children and she was unable to conceive. Members of her family made fun of her and dismissed her emotions. Hannah prayed to God about her bitterness and sadness. God helped her discover His design for her life and then blessed her with a son, Samuel, who was to become a prophet of God. Have students read 1 Samuel 1:1–20 and answer the questions found on the student page. Discuss students' answers as a whole group.

HOW AM I TO DEAL WITH LIFE? (15 minutes)

God's Word tells us that Jesus will help us bear the unjust punishment of those who hurt and make fun of His followers. When we are being ridiculed, it is tempting to fight back. We may, in a weak moment, give in to Satan and speak hastily or harm someone that hurts us. The Scriptures are clear that we are to hold back our anger and pray for our enemy. The Scriptures also reassure us of God's forgiveness during those times of weakness and His promise to bring rescue to His people. It is not easy, but God promises to help and strengthen us.

Guide students through the verses and questions on this section. Help students to understand God's forgiveness and presence in their lives as they face the challenges of living in a fallen world. Have students share their Bible verses of reassurance with the whole group.

CLOSING (10 minutes)

Invite students to write, on newsprint or white board, a list of fears that they or other people have as they live, work, and play with one another. Close by reading Psalm 23, listing a fear students have after each verse. Talk about how the Gospel of Christ, the Good Shepherd, drives out all fear.

LESSON EXTENDERS

✝ Have students record their Bible verses of reassurance onto pieces of poster board. Display them in your classroom or meeting area.

MY LIFE IS IN CHAOS

CHAOTIC LIVES

Think about your daily schedule. Are there times that your schedule seems out of control?

What things in your life seem out of your control right now?

THE UPS AND DOWNS OF LIFE

Read **1 Samuel 1:1–20**.

What was Hannah's life like?

What similarities are there between the chaos in your life and Hannah's?

Explain what Hannah finally did to deal with the pressure in her life.

How did God respond to Hannah?

Where is God's grace evident in Hannah's life?

Where is God's grace evident in your life?

HOW AM I TO DEAL WITH LIFE?

How do these verses relate to Hannah and you as guidance from God?

Proverbs 16:23

Matthew 5:38–39

Romans 12:14–21

Describe your feelings during a time in your life when it seemed everyone was against you.

What was it that moved you to deal directly with your problem?

What words from Scripture have been helpful to you in tough times?

© 2008 Concordia Publishing House. Okay to copy.

STUDENT PAGE 19

28. This Call's For You

1 Samuel 3; 8–11

Lesson Focus

God calls everyone to faith in Jesus; He calls His baptized children to serve Him and enables them to do great things. God's call to faith and service gives people of all ages purpose in life.

AN OFFER YOU CAN'T REFUSE (10 minutes)

Distribute copies of the student page. Choose two sets of paired students to role-play a telephone conversation between friends. The caller uses one of the choices on the student page as an invitation; the friend can respond positively or negatively. The second pair role-plays a different invitation using another choice on the list, but with the opposite response from the first pair. When they finish, ask the class how they would have felt if they had to say no to such a great invitation. What if they could accept it? Today's lesson will study opportunities that God gave to Samuel and Saul and how they each responded. Students will explore opportunities that God gives today and how to respond.

OKAY, I'M LISTENING! (25 minutes)

Read the Bible passages listed on the student page, and discuss the students' responses to the questions.

God warned Samuel about the pending judgment of Eli and his family. The bad news was that Samuel had to tell Eli of God's judgment against him and the coming death of his family. The good news was that God again chose to speak to His people after being silent for a long time. God showed that He still cared about His people.

Read the next passage from later in Samuel's life, and discuss the question.

Samuel prayed to God and told the people everything that the Lord had said; he served as messenger and kept his own feelings between himself and God.

1 Samuel 11:11–15—Good. God helped Saul defeat the Ammonites.

1 Samuel 13:5–14—Evil. Saul disobeyed God by offering the sacrifice in Samuel's place.

1 Samuel 14:47–48—Good. God helped Saul defeat Israel's enemies.

1 Samuel 15:1–11, 24–26—Evil. Saul disobeyed God by keeping plunder from his enemies, and God rejected him as king.

GOD CAN DO THAT . . . THROUGH ME? (15 minutes)

Have students work together in groups to complete this section. Discuss with the class the two types of calls that God gives today, just as He gave to Samuel and Saul, and how each impacts us. Compare these calls to Samuel and Saul. Discuss God's call in your life.

FOLLOWING JESUS (5 minutes)

Close by reading aloud John 10:27–30; then pray together, "Dear Father, thank You for sending Jesus to lead us back to Your loving arms. Forgive us when we run away or follow after other gods. Help us to trust You always. Send us Your Holy Spirit to create and sustain faith in Jesus as our Lord and Savior. Give us courage to answer Your call to serve the Church. Amen." Be especially aware of any youth who want to talk further about a calling from God to service in the Church, and invite such students to talk with you or your pastor.

LESSON EXTENDERS

✝ Direct students to interview their pastor, DCE, deaconess, or Lutheran teacher, and ask, "What is your favorite aspect of church work? What is your least favorite? What made you decide on your vocation?" Discuss the answers next week.

✝ Help students explore the various church-work opportunities available to them. Visit www.whataway.org for more information.

THIS CALL'S FOR YOU

AN OFFER YOU CAN'T REFUSE

Come with me on a trip to Europe (my parents will pay your way).

I'm a contestant on *Who Wants to Be a Millionaire*, and if you'll be my "phone a friend," I'll split my winnings fifty-fifty.

I'm getting a new car for my birthday, and I'll give you my old one for free.

OKAY, I'M LISTENING!

Read **1 Samuel 3**. How would you have reacted if you were Samuel, remembering that you had never heard God's voice before?

....

What did God tell Samuel?

....

Describe the "good news" and "bad news" in God's message.

....

Now read **1 Samuel 8–11**, which outlines Samuel's later life. Discuss:

....

How did Samuel deal with his hurt and anger caused by the Israelites' demand for a king?

....

How did God help him?

....

God answered the people's foolish prayer. Israel received a king, Saul, to govern them. Read the passages below and summarize either the good or the evil that resulted from Saul's reign:

1 Samuel 11:11–15

....

1 Samuel 13:5–14

....

1 Samuel 14:47–48

....

1 Samuel 15:1–11, 24–26

....

GOD CAN DO THAT . . . THROUGH ME?

God calls each of us today, just as He did Samuel and Saul. Use the verses to complete the following statements about how God calls you personally.

God Calls Me to . . .

BELIEVE IN JESUS

This call is for everyone, but eternal life in heaven is given to

....

....

(John 3:16)

The consequences of rejecting this call to faith are

....

....

(Mark 16:16; Matthew 25:41–46)

God promises those who receive Jesus

....

....

(Galatians 5:22–25)

SERVICE IN THE CHURCH

This call is for specific individuals, but through them the gift of eternal life in heaven is offered to

....

....

(2 Thessalonians 2:13–15)

God promises those who serve as professional church workers

....

....

(Isaiah 55:10–11; Ephesians 4:7–16)

© 2008 Concordia Publishing House. Okay to copy.

21. Choosing the Right Tool

1 Samuel 16:1–13

Lesson Focus

God chooses to care for and save His people despite their sinful nature and lack of obedience to His Word.

THE RIGHT TOOL (5 minutes)

Before class, gather a number of tools. You may want to include household items (hammer, screwdriver, etc.), office supplies (stapler, pen, etc.), or whatever is available. As you hold up each tool, ask, "Why would you pick this tool to use?" Talk about each tool, then summarize by saying, "We tend to choose a tool based on its usefulness to us. What about people? How do teens choose friends or people to date? What standards do most people use today?" Allow students time to discuss.

ALL THE WRONG REASONS (20 minutes)

Distribute copies of the student page. Ask students to work in groups of two or three to look up the passages and determine whether or not God chose people based on the quality listed.

When groups have finished, ask, "How many thumbs-up did you come up with?" (There should be none.) "If being chosen by God depended on the qualities listed on your student page, how many of these guys would have been chosen?" (None)

Ask your students to turn to 1 Samuel 16:1–13. After reading the passage together, walk through the questions on the student page as a whole group. Suggested answers include the following: Samuel considered Eliab because of his height and appearance; people look at outward appearances, while God looks at the heart; and this passage doesn't tell us why God chose David, but God looked at what was in his heart. The Holy Spirit came upon David at his anointing.

Explain that this passage does not say why God chose David to be king, only that God did choose David because he had faith and trusted in God. God gave him His Holy Spirit. The Bible makes it clear over and over again that there is nothing in anyone that would cause God to choose him or her. God puts faith in our hearts and uses His faithful children to carry out His plans.

IN HIS SIGHT (15 minutes)

Direct students to this section of the student page. After allowing time for students to record their seven words, ask each to share and explain their choices. Next, ask students to look up the passage listed on the student page and write down the two words suggested there (depending on translation—*holy*, *blameless*).

Ask, "From this passage, what is the standard that God uses to choose people?" Allow students a moment to think and wrestle with the answer if they don't respond right away. Then explain, "God's standard for choosing you is not behavior, looks, talent, faith, or strength. It is nothing that you do or have that makes God choose you. God chooses you, just as He chose David, based on His own love and will. As God's love for you drove Him to give Jesus to die in your place so that you could live with Him forever, God also chooses His children for various types of service in His kingdom, just as He chose David to serve as king.

WOULD GOD CHOOSE? (10 minutes)

Ask students to work in groups of two or three and follow the directions on the student page. When they have finished sharing ideas, close by having them pray for each other.

Choosing the Right Tool

ALL THE WRONG REASONS

Why does God choose people? Look up the passages about the following Bible heroes and circle thumbs-up if it was the reason God chose this person or thumbs-down if it wasn't.

Truthfulness (Abraham—**Genesis 12:10–13**)

Talent/ability (Moses—**Exodus 4:10**)

Faith (the disciples—**Matthew 17:20**)

Strength (Gideon—**Judges 6:15**)

Look up **1 Samuel 16:1–13**.

1. Why did Samuel think Eliab was the one (**v. 6**)?

2. What's the difference between the way people see each other and the way God sees people (**v. 7**)?

3. David had a "fine appearance" (**v. 12**), but that wasn't why God chose him. Why did God choose David?

4. As a result of God's choosing, what happened (**v. 13**)?

IN HIS SIGHT

Think about your parents, relatives, and friends. Make a list of at least seven words (positive or negative) that describe how you think they see you.

Now look at **Ephesians 1:4**. Write two words that describe how God sees you and what you were chosen for in Christ.

WOULD GOD CHOOSE?

A friend asks, "Would God choose me?" Based on what you've read and discussed in this lesson, what would you say?

© 2008 Concordia Publishing House. Okay to copy.

STUDENT PAGE 21

22. THINGS ARE GETTING DIFFICULT

1 Samuel 17:1–54; 18–26

Lesson Focus

Even in the most difficult of circumstances, youth can know that God will never fail or forsake them.

THE MOST DIFFICULT (10 minutes)

Distribute copies of the student page. Have students rank the list of challenges on their own, then share with the group. While we may not understand each challenge listed, David encountered them all while he was a teenager.

YOU THOUGHT YOUR LIFE WAS HARD? (30 minutes)

Since the Scripture lesson is lengthy, focus on David's challenges from his enemies. Before class, read the whole section so you have the big picture. Have student volunteers read the selected verses out loud, asking the group to summarize David's challenge.

David's success was not primarily in battle but in knowing that God would provide what was needed in any situation. As a Christian, knowing *whose* we are makes all the difference: "In everything he did he had great success, because the Lord was with him" (1 Samuel 18:14). Our "success" was accomplished when Jesus conquered sin and death by offering His own life on the cross. His work is applied to us in Baptism through faith. The Lord is with us! God showed His love and His ability to conquer every situation when He sent Jesus to be the sacrifice for our sins. As a result, we courageously face each day, knowing we are His children!

THINK ABOUT IT (5 minutes)

The old computer game Minesweeper forced the player to correctly read warning signs. If not properly understood, "mines" were ignited and the game was over. Those mines are like the challenges in our lives. If we're not properly equipped, there is a major explosion! Talk about the challenges the youth encounter in their daily lives (you might revisit the list in the opening). Have students review the Bible verses listed. Like David, we know that God will never forsake us, that He is greater than any difficulty, and that we will live with Him forever!

CLOSING (5 minutes)

Ask students to think about challenges confronting them or their friends. As a group, pray, mentioning each person by first name: "Dear Lord, we thank You for claiming us as Your children. Help all the people now mentioned to confront and overcome their challenges: *(each person mentions names)*. Give us the strength and courage for all our tasks. In Jesus' name we pray. Amen." Read Romans 8:37–39 together as a group.

LESSON EXTENDERS

✝ A number of people were used by God to help David (Michal, Jonathan, Samuel, Abigail). Ask students to share about some of the people God is using in their lives to provide help.

✝ Think of concrete ways students can offer assistance to someone this week. Perhaps they can do something to help those for whom you prayed. Brainstorm ways to offer real help—boldly but realistically.

Things Are Getting Difficult

THE MOST DIFFICULT

Rank in order of importance those challenges most youth today have to confront.

_____ Caring for parent(s)

_____ Being threatened by bullies

_____ Competing with brother or sister

_____ Having others take or desire your things

_____ Fearing that no place is safe

_____ Wondering when you will eat next

_____ Knowing that friends are lying to you

_____ Needing to "prove" yourself

_____ Trusting that God is at work in your life

_____ *Add your own challenge:* _____

YOU THOUGHT YOUR LIFE WAS HARD?

David experienced it all! As a youth or young adult, David was anointed king, but life didn't get easier. Read about David's challenges:

Giant Goliath—**1 Samuel 17:41–44**

The Philistine army—**1 Samuel 17:1**

Big brother Eliab—**1 Samuel 17:28**

Faithless King Saul—**1 Samuel 18:28–29; 19:1; 22:17; 26:2**

Nabal the fool—**1 Samuel 25:10–11, 21–22, 37–38**

How did David confront each challenge?

1 Samuel 17:47

1 Samuel 18:14

1 Samuel 24:15

THINK ABOUT IT

Read **Deuteronomy 31:6** and **Romans 8:37–39**.

How can Christians prepare to confront the most difficult circumstances?

How does God in Christ offer real help?

© 2008 Concordia Publishing House. Okay to copy.

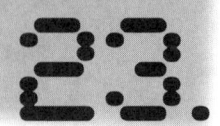

23. Kindness from the King

2 Samuel 9

Lesson Focus

God's gracious way of dealing with His lowly children and an example of lovingly caring for the less fortunate can both be seen in David's action of providing for Mephibosheth.

BETTER THAN SCUM OF THE EARTH (10 minutes)

Distribute copies of the student page. Discuss with students how valuable kindness can be to a person. Help them identify people to whom they can show kindness and ways in which they can do so.

MEPHI-WHO? (15 minutes)

Ask a student volunteer to read the text from 2 Samuel. Students will probably need help pronouncing the main character's name (me-fib´-o-sheth). Allow students time to complete the questions and discuss their answers.

Mephibosheth is Jonathan's son (King Saul's grandson) and is crippled in both feet. He was the dynastic heir to the throne, but David became king. Jonathan and David were very close friends. Jonathan helped protect David from Saul when Saul was trying to kill him. Mephibosheth bowed down to David and said, "Your servant." After David provides for him, Mephibosheth refers to himself as a "dead dog," an indication of lowliness and humility. The degree of Mephibosheth's disability makes it necessary for him to depend on others. David restores the land and property of Saul to Mephibosheth and grants him a place of honor at his table for life.

HOW ARE YOU DOING? (15 minutes)

Work through the questions in this section as a whole group. Help students to see that it is only through faith, by the power of the Spirit, that we are able to overcome our sinful selfishness.

Christians are told by Christ to show kindness "to the least of these" for His sake. In other words, we are to follow Christ's example in caring for others because of what He did for us. Some human reasons for showing kindness include the following: it makes you feel good, it makes other people notice you, it can help ease guilt about other things, and it may help you get a tax break. Human motivation may not always be wrong, but Christian service is motivated primarily by Christ. We can only resist temptation with the help of God because of what Christ did for us.

Give students a few minutes to write their prayers; then invite one or two to share their prayers as your closing.

LESSON EXTENDERS

✝ Plan a service project for your group, such as volunteering to help with the Special Olympics or serving at a senior center or soup kitchen.

Kindness from the King

BETTER THAN SCUM OF THE EARTH

Think about a time someone who didn't even have to pay attention to you did something nice for you. How did it make you feel? How could you reach out in loving-kindness to some unsuspecting person?

MEPHI-WHO?

Read **2 Samuel 9:1–13**.

Who is Mephibosheth (me-fib´-o-sheth)?

What is significant about his father's relationship with David? (See also **1 Samuel 20:12–17** and **42**.)

What is Mephibosheth's response when David calls him in?

Why might the fact that Mephibosheth is crippled in both feet be mentioned?

What does David do for Mephibosheth?

HOW ARE YOU DOING?

Is it easier to show loving-kindness toward others when you are the underdog or when you are near the top of the social order? Why?

To whom and for whose sake do Christians show loving-kindness toward others? (See also **Matthew 25:31–46**.)

What are some human reasons for showing kindness to others? How or when can they be sinful?

Why is it sometimes difficult to get past these things? How are we able to overcome these difficulties?

Write a prayer thanking God for the mercy and loving-kindness He has shown you and asking Him to give you the grace to show loving-kindness to others for Jesus' sake.

© 2008 Concordia Publishing House. Okay to copy.

24. Giving Our Best

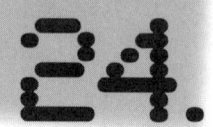

1 Kings 5–8

Lesson Focus

In response to God's gift of salvation through Jesus Christ, participants will be motivated to serve God by giving the best of their time, talents, and money.

OPENING (10 minutes)

Several days before the session, purchase two or three donuts. Allow them to dry out and become stale. Later purchase fresh donuts to share with your class.

When you begin, ask how your students put their faith into action during the past week. Share a personal experience, then allow two or three volunteers to share their experiences. Commend the volunteers and "reward" them with the stale donuts. When they complain about the donuts, ask the class why stale donuts aren't a very good reward. Then bring out the fresh donuts and distribute them. Conclude by saying, "Although we want to thank God, do we give Him leftovers instead of our best? Today we will see how Solomon thanked God by 'giving the best.'"

INTO THE WORD (25 minutes)

Distribute copies of the student page. Read the opening statement and ask the students to read 1 Kings 5:5 and record Solomon's objective. After a moment, allow a student to share a response. Then say, "God had been good to Israel, blessing His people in many ways. In response, Solomon built a temple for Him. Solomon spared no expense. On the student page, look up the Bible references and identify the materials and their uses." After about ten minutes, invite volunteers to share what they have found. (Suggested responses are 1 Kings 5:6—cedars of Lebanon; 5:17—quarry stone; 6:19–20—pure gold; 6:23—olive wood; and 6:34—pine.)

Ask a student to read 1 Kings 6:14–22 aloud. Poll the students for their impressions of the temple. Allow students to share their responses. (Most students will be impressed.) Point out that Solomon gives us an example to follow in giving thanks to the Lord—that we also give the very best.

MY BEST (15 minutes)

Ask the students to consider the ways God has blessed them and record them on the student page. Help those who have trouble responding to see God's goodness by citing specific examples of it, for instance, that He has provided them with salvation through His Son, that He gives them Christian friends like the members of this class, and that He showers them with His constant love and care. Allow the students five minutes to record their responses.

Ask the students to respond to the second question by writing appropriate ways to say thanks for God's blessings. (By giving a portion of their money to the church and others in need, using their talents on servant events, or becoming involved in church activities, among many others.)

Also, challenge them to do something this week to give thanks to God. Request that they record their specific commitment in the space provided.

CLOSING (5 minutes)

Close the session with a prayer, thanking God for the gift of His Son and asking Him to bless their efforts to serve Him in the name of Jesus.

LESSON EXTENDERS

✝ Review Romans 12:3–8 for God's encouragement in using our talents for Him.

✝ Review 2 Corinthians 8:9. What does it say about the source of our giving to God?

Giving Our Best

INTO THE WORD

Solomon wanted to build a temple for the Lord. According to **1 Kings 5:5**, what was his intent?

....

....

Solomon spared no expense in building the temple. He used only the best materials. Check out the Scripture references in the box on the right and identify what materials he used.

Check out **1 Kings 6:14–22**. Write your overall impression of the temple Solomon built in the space below.

....

....

How well did Solomon meet his objective?

....

Solomon built the temple to God's glory in response to the blessings God had given His people.

....

1 Kings 5:6

....

....

1 Kings 5:17

....

....

1 Kings 6:19–20

....

....

1 Kings 6:23

....

....

1 Kings 6:34

....

....

MY BEST

List some of the blessings God has given you:

....

....

What is an appropriate response to those blessings?

....

In what ways could you express your thanks to God during this week? (If you need help, you might check out **Mark 12:41–44; Romans 12:1;** and **Hebrews 13:15–16**.)

....

....

This week I am going to …

....

....

© 2008 Concordia Publishing House. Okay to copy.

25. GOD'S PLANS & PURPOSES

1 Kings 17

Lesson Focus

The God who gives salvation from our sins will also provide us with what we need for our work in His kingdom.

OPENING (5 minutes)

Ask for a volunteer to demonstrate how to make a peanut butter and jelly sandwich. Provide the student with only a plate and knife, and tell him or her to make the sandwich. After he or she protests, discuss the idea that we must have the necessary ingredients to accomplish something. (If you wish, now provide the necessities, and have the student really make the sandwich.) Lead into the lesson, reminding students that God gives us what we need to do His work as well. He supplies the "ingredients" we must have to do His work on earth.

GOD PROVIDES FOR HIS SERVANTS (20 minutes)

In the Old Testament, there are many accounts of God sending prophets to give the people His message. In Elijah's time many people were worshiping false gods, so God sent Elijah to comfort and call back the people. In this account we see God providing care and protection for His servant Elijah.

Distribute copies of the student page. Allow time for the students to work in twos and threes to read the selected Scriptures, and answer the questions from the student page. After you sense that students have completed their work, bring them together for a whole-group discussion of their findings.

God sent a drought, but He protected Elijah by sending him to a different area. Because the people had chosen to worship false gods, God withdrew His spokesman from the land of His unfaithful people while the people suffered for their sinfulness. First God provided water from a brook and food from a bird. Then God sent Elijah to the widow's home. Note how she shared what she had, even though it was very little. Here we are reminded again of Elijah's reliance on God. God performed this first resurrection recorded in Scripture. God provided food, shelter, and wisdom for Elijah. The woman was granted food, safety, and the resurrection of her son. Note how God helped her to rely on Him.

WE ARE SERVANTS (15 minutes)

In addition to our salvation, God gives His servants what they need for their work in His kingdom. Like Elijah and the woman, we are God's servants. As we are called to serve, He not only grants us salvation but also provides us with the resources we need to carry out our mission for Him. This service gives glory to God and helps His people here on earth. Guide students to view themselves as available servants and to see God's support of them. Remind them that our assistance can be offered to pastors, missionaries, teachers, and other workers. Help students to see the value of prayer and financial support for those they don't know personally. Those with whom they do have contact could receive other more personal kinds of support as well.

CLOSING (5 minutes)

Take a few moments to mention by name the missionaries, pastors, Christian teachers, and the like whom students may know. Finish with a prayer of thanks for their work and for God's guidance in our support of them.

LESSON EXTENDERS

✝ Make specific plans to assist and support others as they serve God.

✝ Make a list of other times God helped His servants in the Bible.

God's Plans & Purposes

GOD PROVIDES FOR HIS SERVANTS

Read **1 Kings 17:1**.

What was God's response to the people's idolatry?

How do **verses 2–16** show God's care for Elijah?

In **verse 7,** Elijah's brook dried up. God had a new plan. What was it?

How did the widow respond (**v. 15**)?

Read **verses 17–24**. By whose power was the boy restored to life (**v. 21**)?

In what ways did God provide for Elijah?

How did God provide for the woman who helped Elijah?

WE ARE SERVANTS

How has God helped you to be a servant for Him?

In what ways can we assist others as they serve?

What kinds of service are you capable of providing for those in need?

© 2008 Concordia Publishing House. Okay to copy.

STUDENT PAGE 25

26. TOO PROUD?

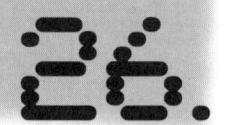

2 Kings 5:1–19

Lesson Focus

Naaman almost passed up a great blessing from God because it came in an *undignified* way. But God's gifts, even Jesus Himself, do not come in dignity, but in humble forms of human flesh and crucifixion.

OPENING (5 minutes)

Put four quarters into an envelope, then into a ziplock bag, and then into a big jar of water you have made as unappealing as possible (by adding harmless ingredients such as food coloring, vinegar, milk, potting soil, and the like). Offer the bag's contents to whomever is willing to reach in with a bare hand and get it. Celebrate with the successful volunteer (and send him or her to clean up). Point out that avoiding things that we feel are messy or undignified could keep us from experiencing blessed surprises.

GETTING INTO SCRIPTURE (15 minutes)

Distribute copies of the student page. Have the students read 2 Kings 5:1–19 and reflect on the situations on the student page (perhaps by writing as Naaman might have written in a journal or by conducting interviews with four students pretending to be Naaman). Challenge the students to consider (1) how they would describe Naaman when he first went to Elisha, (2) what Naaman was expecting, and (3) why Naaman was insulted and angry.

GOING DEEP (15 minutes)

In pairs or small groups, have the students discuss questions 1–3. After about eight minutes, invite volunteers to share responses, incorporating the following comments in the discussion.

(1) Naaman was insulted that Elisha didn't even bother to come to the door. Upset by Elisha's lack of respect and feeling the request was beneath him, Naaman decided to go home. On the way home, God used Naaman's servants to convince him to wash in the Jordan as Elisha had instructed.

(2) The students may have responses in one or more sections of the chart on the student page. Be prepared to share personal responses to "get things going." Do not require sharing.

(3) Accept all answers concerning the Jordan River analogy, but lead the students to see that spiritual healing always comes through God's Word.

PONDERING THE GOSPEL (15 minutes)

Take up each point in turn, reading the student page comments and inviting responses.

(1) Examples might include being critical of Bible class leaders, topics, or participants; looking for faults in worship rather than God's blessings; and seeing concerned friends as "intruding in private affairs."

(2) Most students will be able to identify the encouragement of parents or friends to be active in worship and Bible study.

(3) Answers will vary but might include thanksgiving, recommitment, and reaching out to others to encourage them.

CLOSING (5 minutes)

Invite the students to pray in turn, or ask for prayer requests and pray for the group. Close by singing or speaking the words of "Lord, Whose Love through Humble Service" (*LSB* 848).

LESSON EXTENDERS

✝ See Romans 6:3–4, 11; 1 Corinthians 1:29–31; 2 Corinthians 5:17; Ephesians 3:20; and Philippians 4:13. What do you hear God saying about our power for change?

TOO PROUD?

GETTING INTO SCRIPTURE

Read **2 Kings 5:1–19**. Imagine you are Naaman. What would your thoughts be in the following situations:

• As you first prepare to meet Elisha?

• After Elisha sends word for you to wash in the Jordan River?

• After you have washed in the Jordan and have experienced God's healing?

• As you prepare to meet Elisha a second time?

GOING DEEP

1. What are some characteristics of proud people? How do others react to them? What might be some consequences of pride? How did pride almost cause Naaman to miss God's blessings?

2. Where are you in need of God's healing in spiritual, emotional, physical, or relational aspects of your life?

3. What is your "Jordan River"—the person, place, or activity through which God brings healing into your life?

PONDERING THE GOSPEL

Share your reflections on the thoughts below.

1. Pride attacks us through our sinful nature, but God can change us. Through His Word—Bible study, worship, the counsel of other Christians—God *wants to, can,* and *will* change our hearts, grant us new life in Him, and lead us in the way He desires us to live. How might our sinful nature react to such encounters with God's Word?

2. The Good News is that God persistently pursues Naaman through his servants until Naaman responds in faith. Naaman doesn't *decide* to trust God, but rather He *responds* to God's persistence. See **Romans 10:14–17**. How have you experienced God's persistent love, and how are you responding to His love?

3. How might you *celebrate* God's persistent love this week?

© 2008 Concordia Publishing House. Okay to copy.

STUDENT PAGE 26

27. A CURSE FOR US

2 Kings 11–12

Lesson Focus

King Joash's life was cursed because he disobeyed God's Law. Despite our disobedience against God's Law and the curse that comes as a result, Christ has redeemed us by becoming the curse for us.

OPENING (5 minutes)

Before class, ask two students to help with the following activity. Secretly instruct one student to follow your instructions to the letter and the other to intentionally disregard the instructions you give. In front of the class say, "Using this 8½ x 11-inch piece of paper and the markers I have given you, draw a red circle on the front of the paper and a blue circle on the back of the paper." Hand a piece of paper to each volunteer. After both participants have completed their actions, award the one who followed your instructions with a candy bar. Point out the blessing the student who followed your instructions received.

LIFE OF KING JOASH (15 minutes)

Distribute copies of the student page. Have the students read 2 Kings 11:21–12:2 and 2 Chronicles 24:17–18, 23–25. After reading these verses, have students in small groups answer and reflect on the questions on the student page. Challenge the students to pull out the details of King Joash's life, especially those that occurred after the death of Jehoiada. After about five minutes, invite volunteers to share responses, ensuring that the group realizes that, after Jehoiada died, King Joash turned from God, and God's anger burned against him. God's judgment was rendered on Judah and King Joash, ultimately resulting in the assassination of King Joash.

BLESSINGS VS. CURSES (10 minutes)

Invite students to look at a section of Scripture that reports the perfect obedience God required from the Israelites as a part of the covenant He made with them on Mount Sinai. Discuss the consequences of following the Law versus not following the Law God gave.

In the whole group, ask for a volunteer to read Deuteronomy 11:26–28. Discuss the questions related to these verses so that students will understand that the covenant God made with the Israelites on Mount Sinai was conditional. It required the people to follow His Law to the letter or face the consequences of disobedience. The only way to avoid the consequences is to rely on God's mercy.

WHAT ABOUT THE GOSPEL? (15 minutes)

Have the students respond to the statement on the student page. Ask for a volunteer to read Galatians 3:10–14. Discuss the questions that follow on the student page, helping students understand that we no longer receive the punishment we deserve for not keeping the Law because Christ took that punishment (the curse of the Law) upon Himself.

CLOSING (5 minutes)

Join in singing or reading the words of stanza 1 of "I Lay My Sins on Jesus" (*LSB* 606; *LW* 366). Close by inviting the students to pray in turn, thanking God for giving Jesus to take the punishment of the Law for them.

LESSON EXTENDERS

✝ See Romans 5:6–8; 6:20–23; and Galatians 6:7–9. What do you hear God saying about our state that caused Him to die for us? How might we respond to His love for us?

A CURSE FOR US

LIFE OF KING JOASH

What were you doing when you were seven years old? Imagine that you were to become the leader of your country at that age. On whom would you rely for guidance?

Read **2 Kings 11:21–12:2** and **2 Chronicles 24:17–18, 23–25**.

Joash became king of Judah at the age of seven. What were the highlights of his life? Who instructed Joash as he became king?

What happened to King Joash after the death of Jehoiada, and why did it happen?

BLESSINGS VS. CURSES

God's Word is clear regarding the results of following His Law as opposed to disobeying His Law. Based on **Deuteronomy 11:26–28**, what is the result of following, as opposed to disobeying, God's Law?

Based on these verses, is there any way for those who disobey God's commands to avoid facing the curse?

WHAT ABOUT THE GOSPEL?

What is your reaction to the following statement?

I am a poor miserable sinner. I cannot or will not ever be able to obey every letter of God's Law. I feel as if I have no hope.

Read **Galatians 3:10–14**. According to these verses, on whom has the curse intended for us been placed? Based on His obedience to the Law, what did Jesus deserve to receive? What did He receive instead?

What blessing is ours because He became a curse for us?

How do these verses change your reaction to the statement above?

© 2008 Concordia Publishing House. Okay to copy.

28. Dealing with Doubt

2 Kings 18:1–20:11

Lesson Focus

When we experience doubt, God turns us to the solid foundation of Jesus Christ and the certain truth of His Word, where God's constant love and care are revealed to us.

OPENING (10 minutes)

Invite the students to play "I doubt it." Each person thinks of a "fact"—either something that sounds fantastic but is true ("Concrete can float") or something that sounds credible but is not true ("Men have more teeth than women"). Start the game by announcing your "fact." Any student can challenge your statement, saying, "I doubt it." If your statement isn't true, the "doubter" scores a point. If it is true, you get the point. If the statement is untrue, but no one challenges it, everyone but you loses a point. Rotate to other players until everyone has had a turn.

Distribute copies of the student page, and discuss the statements about doubt. Help the students to recognize that faith is God's *gift* to us through the Holy Spirit. It is not diminished by doubt (1 John 3:19–20).

DOUBTS OF A FAITHFUL KING (20 minutes)

Divide the class into three groups, and assign each a portion of 2 Kings from the student page. Invite each group to read the verses indicated and respond to the questions. After about ten minutes, have the groups report their responses, adding these comments:

2 Kings 18:1–25; 19:1–7

(1) Hezekiah was obviously a strong follower of God (18:3–7).

(2) The faith of Hezekiah and his subjects is challenged by the boasting Assyrian commander, who claims the destruction of Jerusalem is God's will (2 Kings 18:25).

2 Kings 19:14–19, 32–37

(3) Hezekiah prays to God, seeking reassurance. Through the prophet Isaiah, God sends word that the Assyrians will fail.

2 Kings 20:1–11

(4) Hezekiah is ill and near death. Even Isaiah tells Hezekiah to expect death.

(5) Hezekiah again prays to God with immediate results. God grants Hezekiah another fifteen years of life and kingship. At Hezekiah's request, God provides additional assurance by causing a shadow on the stairs to move backward, that is, God moves the sun backward in the sky to demonstrate His power to act on Hezekiah's behalf.

DOUBTING DISCIPLES (15 minutes)

Read this paragraph on the student page. Then direct the students to consider what parts of their lives create doubt and ways God addresses those doubts. After about five minutes, invite the students to pair up with a friend to complete the questions. (Often our friends can see and testify to God's actions in our lives more clearly than we ourselves.)

SIGNS FROM GOD (5 minutes)

Direct the students to read the final paragraph. Invite comments.

CLOSING (5 minutes)

Lead the students in this prayer: "Thank You, Lord, for our faith in Christ. Thanks also for the many sources of assurance You provide in our lives—especially for Your Word and Sacraments and for the messages of assurance You bring us through Christian friends. Support us in every moment of doubt. In Jesus' name we pray. Amen."

LESSON EXTENDERS

✝ Create a "Doubters Hall of Fame." List, illustrate, and locate the Bible passages that describe people of faith who doubted.

Dealing With Doubt

"I do believe; help me overcome my unbelief!" (Mark 9:24)

What do you think about this statement? Are faith and doubt compatible?

DOUBTS OF A FAITHFUL KING

Check out the doubts of Hezekiah in these sections of 2 Kings.

Read **2 Kings 18:1–25**.

1. How would you characterize Hezekiah and his faith?

2. What might Hezekiah be doubting in this passage? Why?

Read **2 Kings 19:14–19, 32–37**.

3. How does God reassure Hezekiah?

Read **2 Kings 20:1–11**.

4. What might Hezekiah be doubting in this passage? Why?

5. How does God reassure Hezekiah?

DOUBTING DISCIPLES

Every faithful follower of Jesus is also an imperfect human being. At times we question what God is doing in our lives, just like Hezekiah, Thomas, and many others. In what areas of your life—past, present, or future—is there doubt? How does God address your doubts in His Word or in your world?

SIGNS FROM GOD

In times past, God has given His people signs to strengthen their faith—the movement of the shadow on Hezekiah's stairs, Jesus' physical appearance to Thomas after the resurrection. Jesus gives us signs, too—especially His body and blood in the bread and wine of Holy Communion and the water in Baptism. They are tangible reminders of His constant love.

© 2008 Concordia Publishing House. Okay to copy.

STUDENT PAGE 28

29. FOR SUCH A TIME AS THIS

Book of Esther

Lesson Focus

God preserved Israel as a part of His plan to offer salvation through the coming Messiah. By His coming, we receive forgiveness and life eternal.

OPENING (5 minutes)

Ask students what it means to "be in the right place at the right time." Encourage them to provide examples of when they have been in the right place at the right time or someone else has been there for them.

RECAP THE STORY (15 minutes)

Distribute copies of the student page. Ask for five volunteers, and assign a character to each (King, Esther, Mordecai, Haman, Narrator). Have them read aloud the key points of the Book of Esther, using the outline on the student page. Afterward, ask students what the key ideas are from this biblical narrative. What does it teach them about God? About being a disciple of Christ? Affirm all answers. Encourage youth to see Mordecai's unwavering faith as he refused to break the First Commandment and bow down to Haman (3:5) and as he views Esther as being placed in the right place at the right time (4:12–17) in order to preserve God's chosen people. Esther's faith is seen as she submits to God's plan and prepares herself through fasting and prayer (4:15–17).

THE FUTURE PROTECTED (20 minutes)

Assign the seven passages to various individuals or groups of students. Point out that three of the passages involve looking up two or three separate references. Ask students to read their passage(s) and answer the three questions. When completed, ask the students to read or summarize each passage and provide opportunity for response. Possible responses: Genesis 12:1–2—Israel is blessed, Haman is "cursed," Christians receive the blessings of God through Jesus. Deuteronomy 7:6—God cared for His chosen people by not allowing Haman's plot to go through; 1 Peter 2:9 indicates that Christians are now God's chosen people, and the Church is His holy nation. Nehemiah 9:30–31 and Jeremiah 5:15–19—The Book of Esther is about the Jews in exile in Assyria, yet the Lord is still caring for them; today, God's ultimate care and mercy are given to us through Jesus Christ. Isaiah 49:6—In Esther we see God's "keeping" of the Israelites, and Esther 8:17 indicates that many became God's people when they witnessed what God did for the Jews. Luke 2:30–32 tells us that Christ is the ultimate fulfillment of the "light . . . to the Gentiles." Although Jesus was an Israelite, He came for all people. Jeremiah 23:3–6—God preserved Israel so that Jesus/Salvation could come to God's people. Christians know that this prophecy has been fulfilled in Jesus. Jeremiah 31:31–33—God preserved the Jews in order to establish a new and lasting covenant with them; Hebrews 8:8–9—Christians know that God has fulfilled this prophecy and that they live under this New Testament covenant.

A TIME FOR EVERYTHING (10 minutes)

Provide quiet time for students to reflect on the three questions. Ask for volunteers to share their responses.

LESSON EXTENDERS

✝ Use a Bible dictionary or encyclopedia to learn about the Jewish festival of Purim (Esther 9:18–23).

FOR SUCH A TIME AS THIS

RECAP THE STORY

Review the story of Esther by reading the following passages in the order provided:

King Xerxes: **1:1–3, 10–12, 19**

Mordecai: **2:5–6**

Esther: **2:7, 17**

Mordecai: **2:21–23**

Haman: **3:1–2, 5–6**

Mordecai: **4:1**

Esther: **4:5**

Mordecai: **4:7–8**

Esther: **4:9–11**

Mordecai: **4:12–14**

Esther: **4:15–16; 5:1–4**

King Xerxes: **6:1–3, 10**

Haman: **6:11–14**

Esther: **7:1–6**

Haman: **7:9–10**

Narrator: **9:5, 10, 23–28**

THE FUTURE PROTECTED

God had a plan for the people of Israel that spanned centuries into the future. Look up the Scripture passages below, and consider the following questions for each passage. (Note that each passage may not apply to all three questions.)

How does the passage apply to the Jews in the time of Esther?
How does the passage speak to God's preservation of Israel in times past?
How does the passage relate to Christians today?

1) **Genesis 12:1–2**

2) **Deuteronomy 7:6**; also look up **1 Peter 2:9**

3) **Nehemiah 9:30–31**

4) **Jeremiah 5:15–19**

5) **Isaiah 49:6**; compare with **Esther 8:17** and **Luke 2:30–32**

6) **Jeremiah 23:3–6**

7) **Jeremiah 31:31–33**; compare with **Hebrews 8:8–9**

A TIME FOR EVERYTHING

What do you think about when you consider how God planned Christmas (the birth of the Savior of both Jews and Gentiles) for thousands of years?

What can this lesson teach us about God's plans for His Church?

Do you think God has plans for you? What might they be?

© 2008 Concordia Publishing House. Okay to copy.

STUDENT PAGE 29

30. WHOLLY FORGIVEN?

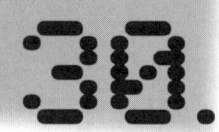

Isaiah 6:1–8; 9:1–6

Lesson Focus

"Holy, holy, holy" describes our majestic God. Isaiah's "woe to me" in God's presence portrays a humble response to God's righteousness. Yet God comes to us not in indescribable majesty but in the humility of the Christ Child. In faith we respond to God's mercy: "Lord, send me!"

OPENING (5 minutes)

Bring in newspaper photos, CD cases, or other items that show pictures of important or well-known individuals (such as the president of the United States, a famous musician, or a movie or sports star). Show the pictures to the students and discuss this question: In whose presence would you be extremely nervous? The president of a country? A celebrity? Discuss other possibilities. Then ask, "How comfortable are you in God's presence?" Allow students to respond and explain why.

A HOLY VISION (15 minutes)

Distribute copies of the student page. Have the students read Isaiah 6:1–8 and name several visual images found in the text. Discuss what is spoken and sung in God's presence: "Holy, holy, holy" and Isaiah's "woe to me." Challenge the students to consider why Isaiah would respond in this situation with humility.

God is seated on a throne, wearing a robe with a long train. The seraphs had wings, faces, feet, and could fly. They were speaking to each other. Sin is forgiven in this powerful image. God is still holy; we sing heavenly praises. In the confession we acknowledge our woefulness.

THE SIN SOLUTION (15 minutes)

Allow students to work in pairs to discuss the first two questions from this section on the student page. After a few minutes, allow students to share their findings with the group. Discuss the damaging effects of sin not only on relationships but also on us as physical, emotional, and spiritual creatures. Sin is forgiven at the cross and extended to the believer for Christ's sake. By rights we deserve God's wrath and punishment.

Read Isaiah 9:1–6. God has given us Jesus, His Son. Briefly describe and discuss the names of Jesus included in verse 6. God solves our sin problem by sending Jesus as a child, in humility, to save us from our sins through His perfect obedience to the Law. Encourage students to discuss each of Jesus' names in turn and provide a biblical example when this characteristic was demonstrated or a way it is real for the students today.

JOY IN FORGIVENESS (15 minutes)

Discuss the questions as a whole group. Help students to understand that as we daily remember our Baptism, regularly participate in the Lord's Supper, and immerse ourselves in God's Word, we can be assured of God's forgiveness for us personally. Like Isaiah, our faith response to God's love for us is "Here am I. Send me!" God's Spirit, dwelling in us, motivates us to serve others in joy and thankfulness. Answers will vary, but some might include helping family or friends, attending worship, and watching for opportunities to help someone in need.

CLOSING (5 minutes)

Invite students to share prayer requests with the group. If possible, write down and photocopy the requests for students to remember in their private prayers during the week.

LESSON EXTENDERS

✝ Isaiah's awestruck response in the presence of God parallels other biblical individuals who received God's Word. Can you think of anyone else in Scripture who responds in this way? (Mary, Luke 1:28–38; Abraham, Genesis 22:1–8.)

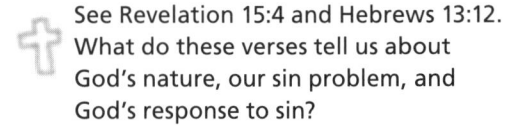

✝ See Revelation 15:4 and Hebrews 13:12. What do these verses tell us about God's nature, our sin problem, and God's response to sin?

WHOLLY FORGIVEN?

A HOLY VISION

Read **Isaiah 6:1–8**. Describe what you see as you read these verses.

How does Isaiah describe the Lord?

....

What are the seraphim? What do they look like?

....

What is said or sung in the presence of God?

....

Why do we include "Holy, holy, holy" in our Communion liturgy?

....

Where do we see the "woe to me" in the Divine Service?

....

THE SIN SOLUTION

Think of a time when sin created a division between you and another person. When was the sin forgiven? Did that difficulty damage the relationship? If so, how?

....

Now think about your sin, which separates you from the holiness of God. How would you expect a just and righteous God to respond to sin?

....

Read **Isaiah 9:1–6**. How does God respond to our sinful state?

....

What do these names tell us about God's attitude toward us?

....

JOY IN FORGIVENESS

In humility and meekness, Jesus took the punishment for our guilty sentence from the court of God's justice. Today, how does God show His forgiveness to you?

....

Isaiah's humble response is not only "Woe to me," but "Here am I. Send me." What motivates him to respond with such joy and action?

....

How might you respond to God's love and forgiveness in joy and action this week?

....

© 2008 Concordia Publishing House. Okay to copy.

STUDENT PAGE 30

31. THE GREATEST POWER

Daniel 3

Lesson Focus
Although we may experience suffering in our lives, God's powerful love sustains us in all suffering.

OPENING (5 minutes)

Have students go through a variety of magazines looking for any symbols or images of power. Have them talk about the pictures, commenting on the type of power represented, and discuss which is the greatest.

GETTING INTO SCRIPTURE (15 minutes)

Do a dramatic reading of Daniel 3:1–30. Assign volunteers to the parts of narrator and the various other characters who speak. Ask students to make lists of items that involve power as defined on the student page.

GOING DEEPER (20 minutes)

Use the questions from the student page to further discuss the text. Points to bring out in discussion:

In the ancient world the king had ultimate power. The king had no power over fire but had to have men build the fire. The king had power over these men, but God has ultimate power over all. The king felt that his power and authority were being publicly challenged. He became furious because three Jewish foreigners saw their God as more powerful and worthy of their attention than their dedication to him. Shadrach, Meshach, and Abednego's response reveals their faith in God, who defends His people differently. Perhaps they are saying that they won't get caught up in an earthly power struggle with him because they know that in the end power does not involve any form of "might" or "force" but is hidden in love, which comes from their God.

The "good news" of what God is doing is indicated in verses 24–25. A fourth person, who "looks like a son of the gods," is present. God is with them in the midst of difficulty and pain. There is no indication in the Scriptures that we will not have to suffer. In fact, the opposite is true. Isaiah 43:2–3 says, "*When* you pass through the waters" and "*when* you walk through the fire." It does not say *if* you will . . . Christ reminds us that we bear a cross *for the sake of the Gospel.*

A "CROSS" WORD PUZZLE (10 minutes)

Have students complete the "cross" word puzzle and discuss the question. In 1 Corinthians 1:18, note that Paul refers to "The message of the cross . . . the power of God." The cross is power. Shadrach, Meshach, and Abednego would not have known specifics about the cross of Jesus, but as a part of God's chosen people, they looked forward to the fulfillment of His plan of salvation in the Messiah, Jesus. And as God's people, they understood the way of the cross. The only way that this willingness to give up their lives for God could happen with anyone (even today) is if God empowered them by His Spirit. Note that the king also gives a powerful witness to God as a result of their faithful witness to Him.

CLOSING (5 minutes)

Close with prayer, being sure to include petitions for those who may be suffering in any way.

THE GREATEST POWER

GETTING INTO SCRIPTURE

Powerful People

Actions That Involve Power

People Having Little Power

Places Where Power Is Involved

GOING DEEPER:

Who had greater power?   King or People

Which had the greater power?   King or Fire

Who had the greater power?   King or the Three Jewish Men

Why do you think the king became so furious?

What words indicate the men's confidence in God?

Who has the greatest power?

Where do you see the Gospel in this Old Testament story?

How do the words of **Isaiah 43:2–3** echo the truth about God in this story?

A "CROSS" WORD PUZZLE

Across: 1 Corinthians 1:18 "The message of the _____ is foolishness to those who are perishing, but to us who are being saved it is the power of God."

Down: Mark 8:34 [Jesus said to His disciples,] "If anyone would come after Me, he must deny himself and take up his _____ and follow Me."

What do you think is meant by each of these *cross* phrases in these passages?

© 2008 Concordia Publishing House. Okay to copy.

32. A LOVE FOR ALL

Book of Jonah

Lesson Focus

The story of Jonah demonstrates God's unfailing love and mercy extended to all people, including those who act as His enemies. God's forgiveness is free to all who call on Him.

OPENING (5 minutes)

Ask students the following questions, and tell them they must choose one of the two options. "Would you rather see your worst enemy punished for his wrongdoing or see him forgiven and not held accountable for what he has done?" "Would you rather spend three days in the belly of a fish or see your worst enemy forgiven?" Ask students why they chose what they did.

BUT THEY HURT ME! (15 minutes)

Distribute copies of the student page. Ask students to record their reactions to the situations given. After a few minutes, ask volunteers to share their responses.

Say, "There will be times in life when we are asked to do something for our 'enemies' that we do not think is fair or that we do not want to do. Today we look at what happened when God asked Jonah to go to Nineveh to tell the wicked people there to repent."

YOU WANT ME TO DO WHAT?! (10 minutes)

Ask students to share their response to the first question. After a few responses have been shared, ask for a volunteer to read Jonah 1:1–2 and 3:1–2. Discuss the questions, helping students understand that God commanded Jonah to go to Nineveh to preach against it so that the people might turn from their great sin of disobedience and unbelief. The Ninevites were enemies of the people of Israel. Jonah did not want to deliver God's message of repentance and grace.

YOU DID WHAT, GOD?! (10 minutes)

Ask for a volunteer to read Jonah 4:1–11. Discuss the questions found on the student page. Encourage students to visualize living at the time of Jonah and the people of Israel as they discuss the last question. Remind students that Nineveh was the capital of Assyria, an enemy to Israel that sought to reduce the size of Israel and to control its internal affairs. God withdrew His punishment, and Jonah felt humiliated and angry at God.

WHAT DO YOU WANT ME TO DO? (5 minutes)

Ask for volunteers to read 1 Timothy 2:1–6 and Ezekiel 18:21–23. Discuss the questions, making sure that students understand that only by the power of God's Spirit can we come to faith and receive redemption through the work of Jesus Christ. Remind them of God's desire for all people to be saved. Help students make a list of ways they can take the message of God's grace to others.

CLOSING (5 minutes)

Join in singing or reading the words of "Hark, the Voice of Jesus Calling" (*LSB* 826/827; *LW* 318). Close with a circle prayer. Ask students to pray for one of their enemies (without mentioning names) and for God's guidance as they reach out to this person with the Gospel message.

LESSON EXTENDERS

✝ Write a letter to a missionary, offering encouragment for his or her efforts of sharing God's Word with all His people.

✝ Prepare a list of Scripture verses on forgiveness, such as Ezekiel 18:21–23 and 2 Peter 3:9, in a form suitable for a pamphlet, and distribute them to individuals at local correctional facilities.

A Love for All

BUT THEY HURT ME!
Briefly describe the feelings resulting from the following situations:

Your brother/sister went into your bedroom without your permission and broke your iPod. Your parents refuse to punish him/her, and tell you if you want a new iPod, you will have to replace it yourself.

....
....
....
....
....

There are a few students at school who are always arguing or fighting with others. These conflicts keep you from focusing on studies, friendships, or extracurricular activities. The principal wants you to tell these students that they need to improve their behavior.

....
....
....
....
....
....

YOU WANT ME TO DO WHAT?!
Have you ever been asked to do something you thought was completely ridiculous? Explain.

....
....

Read **Jonah 1:1–2** and **3:1–2**.
What did God command Jonah to do?

....

Why do you think Jonah ran to Tarshish instead of following the command of God?

....

YOU DID WHAT, GOD?!
Read **Jonah 4:1–11**.
What did God do when the Ninevites repented?

....

What was Jonah's reaction to God's action toward the Ninevites?

....

If you were Jonah, how would you have responded to God's action toward the Ninevites? Why?

....
....

WHAT DO YOU WANT ME TO DO?
Read **1 Timothy 2:1–6** and **Ezekiel 18:21–23**.
According to these verses, whom does God want to be saved?

....

Who has made it possible for all to be saved?

....

What are we to do for *all* people, including our enemies?

....
....

© 2008 Concordia Publishing House. Okay to copy.

33. The Plan

Luke 1:5–25

Lesson Focus

God's plan of salvation defies our human logic, yet through His plan, all of humankind is offered salvation through the death and resurrection of Christ.

HOW I'D SAVE THE WORLD (10 minutes)

Begin the lesson by telling your class, "I want each one of you to take a couple of minutes to come up with a plan to save the world." Give your students time to think; then ask each student to share his or her plan. Encourage the class to discuss the various ideas presented and how effective their plan would be at actually saving the world. After a few minutes say, "What if I said, 'I'll just kill one person, and the world will be saved'? Do you think your non-Christian friends would think that was crazy? Sometimes we forget what a scandal God's plan to save the world is, but today's Bible lesson reminds us that, as wild as it is, it is based on historical facts that have real meaning for our lives today."

JUST THE FACTS (15 minutes)

Distribute student pages, and ask students to look up Luke 1:5–25. Ask students to follow the directions in this section on the student page. When students have finished filling in their sheets, ask, "Which of these facts do you think are most important and why? Why is this particular story important in God's plan of salvation? Why do you think this story is included here? Why is it important that the Bible contains so many historical dates, places, and facts?"

Explain that this story of the birth of John the Baptist is God's way of continuing to unfold His plan of salvation. Luke records this story so we can understand who John was and what he was sent to do. It is an important story because it fulfills prophecy (Matthew 17:9–13) and shows how God is involved in working His plan in and through the daily lives of His people. Knowing the facts of Scripture reminds us that God forgives sin and gives eternal life through the historical, factual death and resurrection of Jesus. God's gift of salvation is not a faint dream, but a real hope anchored in the real life and work of His Son on our behalf.

A PLAN TO SHARE THE FACTS (15 minutes)

Direct students' attention to this section of the student page. Invite them to list the name of a friend who is not a Christian. Then ask students to think about that person and write down any "openings" they can think of. Openings are hurts, fears, or challenges in a friend's life that might make him or her open to the Gospel. For instance, someone may be struggling with loneliness or depression, their parents' divorce, or even something like a big test coming up. Next, ask students to think of Jesus Christ's life and words. What acts of Jesus or Bible verses come to mind that might apply to their friend's situation? Encourage students to work together in sharing friends' situations and brainstorming possible Gospel "facts" that they might share. Ask them to record these facts on the student page.

CLOSING (5 minutes)

Wrap up your time by asking class members to pray for the friends they listed on their paper. Close by reciting the Apostles' Creed together.

THE PLAN

JUST THE FACTS

Sometimes God's plan for saving the world is so familiar to us that we take the facts for granted. Take a few minutes to review **Luke 1:5–25**, and then fill in the blanks.

The main two people: .... and .... (vv. 5–7)

The place: .... (vv. 8–9)

The messenger: .... (vv. 11, 19)

The Plan

Name: .... (vv. 13)

Description: .... (vv. 14–15)

His purpose: .... (vv. 16–17)

The proof: .... (vv. 19–20)

The witnesses: .... (vv. 21–22)

The testimony .... (vv 23–25)

A PLAN TO SHARE THE FACTS

Friend's name

....

Openings (hurts, fears, challenges):

....

....

Five facts about Jesus that my friend needs to hear:

1. ....

2. ....

3. ....

4. ....

5. ....

© 2008 Concordia Publishing House. Okay to copy.

STUDENT PAGE 33

34. PUZZLED

Luke 1:26–56

Lesson Focus

God chooses us according to His purpose and timing to carry out His plans. We can serve God even though we sometimes don't fully understand what He is doing, because He strengthens us through the Holy Spirit.

PUZZLE PICTURE
(15 minutes)

Distribute copies of the student page and a piece of a large puzzle (five hundred pieces or more) to each person in the room. Ask people to draw the rest of the puzzle based on the piece they are holding. Don't let anyone see the puzzle box. Students may draw on the back of their student page. You may add a step by working in breakout groups using everybody's puzzle pieces together. Discuss the questions from the student page.

MARY'S PUZZLE PIECE
(20 minutes)

Have students read the text and respond to the questions on the student page. These are some possible answers:

We never see God's entire plan, but Scripture shows us what God has revealed about His plan of salvation. He revealed some things to Mary, but not everything. God sent the angel not only to calm Mary's fears, but also to help her understand how she fit into the big plan. It was necessary for her to know that she was going to carry the Son of God in her womb before she was married. "Highly favored" meant that God out of His divine grace chose Mary to serve Him. It may have frightened Mary since she knew she was unworthy to serve Him.

Mary was not sinless. However, the Holy Spirit had given her a strong faith. When faced with the challenge of serving God, Mary was willing to do whatever God asked of her. Her attitude reflected a spirit of joyful service. God can do anything. He rejoices when His people willingly serve without question. It is *not* our attitude or willingness to serve that gives us favor in God's eyes. Like Mary, we find favor in God's eyes only because of His grace in sending Jesus to be our Savior. Mary knew God could do whatever He wanted. Gabriel answered by showing us that God is not limited to what we can understand. It would be a divine mystery.

Jesus had to be true God and man to accomplish His work of salvation. (As true man, He would keep the Law perfectly in our place and be our substitute. As true God, He would be able to pay for the sins of the world through His suffering, death, and resurrection.) If Jesus had been born under normal circumstances to a human mother and father, He would have been sinful, without the ability to save us. So as part of God's plan of salvation, Jesus becomes incarnate in Mary through the power of the Holy Spirit, becoming both true God and true man.

When Gabriel told Mary about Elizabeth, it probably gave her comfort and peace to have another person to talk with. That may be one reason why Mary immediately went to Elizabeth's house. Mary may have been there when John was born.

NOTHING IS IMPOSSIBLE
(15 minutes)

Discuss the questions from the student page with the whole group.

Mary would have a baby even though she had never had sexual intercourse, while Elizabeth would have a baby even though she was past the age of childbearing.

God will never leave us or forsake us. He will never give us more than we can handle with His strength. He promises that all things will work together for good for those who love God and are called according to His purpose. The final outcome is victory.

Close with a prayer.

PUZZLED

PUZZLE PICTURE

Could you draw a detailed, accurate picture from a single puzzle piece?

After trying, how accurate were you?

Would it help to have a few more pieces that fit together?

Does it help to have the picture described to you?

Once you see the big picture, why is it easier to see how the small piece fits into it?

MARY'S PUZZLE PIECE

Read **Luke 1:26–38**.

God has a big plan to save the whole world. Do you think teenage Mary understood how she would be a part of that? Why?

What did God send the angel Gabriel to explain to Mary?

What does "highly favored" mean? What do you think Mary thought it meant? Why did that trouble Mary?

In **verse 30** the angel says again that Mary has found favor with God. Does that mean she was sinless? (**Romans 3:23** may help.) Read **verse 38**. What was Mary's attitude toward serving God? Is having this kind of attitude how we find favor in God's eyes?

Mary's question did not ask if this miracle would happen, but *how* it would happen. What is the difference? What was Gabriel's answer?

Why did Jesus have to be born of a woman according to God's plan? Why was it important for Jesus to be true God?

How might Mary have felt when she heard of her cousin Elizabeth?

NOTHING IS IMPOSSIBLE

What were the two miracles God was doing in Mary and Elizabeth?

Mary was just a young teenager, maybe fourteen to sixteen years old, when she received the news. Age is not a factor in God's love. How might God use you for His will?

When God chooses people for His plan, they may not see and understand everything He is doing. What does God promise to His people? (See **Hebrews 13:5**; **1 Corinthians 10:13**; and **Romans 8:28**.)

© 2008 Concordia Publishing House. Okay to copy.

35. THE RIGHT TIME

Luke 1:57–80; 3:1–18

Lesson Focus

The life of John the Baptizer demonstrates the fulfillment of God's promised covenant with Israel.

OPENING (5 minutes)

Ask students to share a time when something they wanted took a long time to come about, yet, when it finally occurred, the timing seemed perfect, and they were glad it had not come earlier.

THE RIGHT TIME FOR A NEW COVENANT (10 minutes)

Distribute copies of the student page. Ask someone to read the introduction aloud. Ask all of the students to turn to Luke 1:57–66, skim the passage, and briefly discuss the context of John's birth and his naming. Have students read 1:67–75 individually or in breakout groups and answer the two questions. Discuss as a whole group. Responses: The Holy Spirit gave Zechariah the understanding that the events were a fulfillment of God's promise of earlier prophecies; verses 69 and 72 connect the Jeremiah passages when they refer to David's house and God's covenant.

TIME TO PREPARE THE WAY FOR THE LORD (15 minutes)

Assign the passages regarding John the Baptizer to students or groups of students. Ask each to read the passage and be ready to share their insights. Answers: 1:66—The Lord's hand was with him; 1:76—Will be called a prophet of the Most High; John will prepare the way for the Lord; 1:77—Gives people the knowledge of salvation through the forgiveness of sins; 3:2—Spoke what God told him; 3:3—Traveled, preaching Baptism and repentance; 3:4—Preparing the way for the Lord (note that this is a fulfillment of a prophecy in Isaiah 40:3–5); 3:6—Proclaims salvation for all, both Jews and Gentiles; 3:16—Tells of the One to come; 3:18—Exhorted the people and preached the Good News to them.

THE RIGHT TIME FOR SALVATION (10 minutes)

Assign the four passages about Jesus to students or groups of students. Ask them to read the passage and be ready to share their answers aloud. Responses: 1:69—Jesus is the "horn of salvation" promised to Israel; 1:78–79—Jesus is the "rising sun" who will shine on us and guide our feet; 1:32—The angel tells Mary that Jesus will be "the Son of the Most High," while 1:76 informs us that John will be "called a prophet of the Most High"; 3:15–17—Jesus is more powerful than John, will baptize with the Holy Spirit and fire, and has come to grant eternal life or death.

NOW IS THE TIME (10 minutes)

Allow time for students to answer the questions on their own. Share responses. (Joseph and Esther spared their people from physical harm and death; the Messiah saves both body and soul from hell.) Prepare a poster board with a clock (or another symbol representing time) drawn on it. Ask students to write their responses to the 1 Corinthians passage on the poster board. Close in prayer.

LESSON EXTENDERS

✝ Use a concordance to look up and discuss Old Testament prophesies concerning Christ and John.

THE RIGHT TIME

THE RIGHT TIME FOR A NEW COVENANT

About six hundred years have passed since Jeremiah prophesied that God would "raise up to David a righteous Branch, a King" (**Jeremiah 23:5**) and "make a new covenant with the house of Israel" (**Jeremiah 31:31**). Zechariah refers to these promises of God in his song of praise. Read **Luke 1:67–75**, and respond to the following questions:

From where does Zechariah gain his understanding of the events of his time?

How does this song of praise connect to the above-mentioned verses from Jeremiah?

TIME TO PREPARE THE WAY FOR THE LORD

Read the following passages from the Gospel of Luke, and describe what they tell you about John the Baptist:

1) **1:66**

2) **1:76**

3) **1:77**

4) **3:2**

5) **3:3**

6) **3:4**

7) **3:6**

8) **3:16**

9) **3:18**

THE RIGHT TIME FOR SALVATION

Read the following verses from the Gospel of Luke, and discover what they teach about Jesus.

1) **1:69**

2) **1:78–79**

3) **1:32** (compare with **1:76** above)

4) **3:15–17**

NOW IS THE TIME

Compare how God saved His people through Joseph and Esther and how He is about to save them through the Messiah.

How does **1 Corinthians 2:6** relate to us today?

36. THE SAME OLD STORY

Luke 2:1–20

Lesson Focus

The traditions of Christmas help us to teach the story about God's plan of salvation while focusing our attention on God's grace and our eternal salvation.

CHRISTMAS TRADITIONS (10 minutes)

Gather the students around a Christmas tree, wreath, or manger scene. You may even go into the sanctuary or a quiet place for this special occasion. Distribute copies of the student page and discuss the questions from this section.

READING THE STORY (25 minutes)

One of the great Christmas traditions is the reading of the Christmas story. Ask students to quietly listen as a volunteer(s) reads the Christmas story in Luke 2:1–20. Guide a discussion of the questions from the student page, noting the following:

Help the students to see God at work in the subtle and small details in the Christmas story. Peace comes through God's plan of salvation for all people, but especially in the way God turns His wrath from us toward His Son. Jesus became human to save us, and He knows what it is like to be human. When God sent the angels to the shepherds, He was sending a clear message that Jesus was coming for everyone, including the poor and the humble. The shepherds certainly responded in a positive way.

Jesus' humble beginnings show that His work is done by the power of the Holy Spirit and not through typical worldly strategies. By being humble, poor, and weak, Jesus shows that God's plan of salvation is counterintuitive, even foolish (1 Corinthians 1:18). God provides the power to make the plan work. The purpose of Jesus' ministry was to bring salvation through His death and resurrection to all people. It is free to everyone who believes.

PASSING ON THE STORY (15 minutes)

Encourage students to understand that even though most of them have heard this story, perhaps all of their lives, we continue to listen to it because it clearly presents God's love for us. The traditional Christmas story is loved and recited all over the world. Even though much of Christmas is commercialized, we can use the power of this traditional story to teach the world about Jesus. The story is made complete at the cross and in the empty tomb.

Just as the shepherds went throughout the city telling the story of the good news, we, too, have the power through the Holy Spirit to announce that real peace comes to us through Jesus' birth. What is that peace? Jesus' death is the great act that brings peace between God and us. It is the assurance that God is with us here and now and guides His children to eternity through faith in Jesus Christ. God has everything under control, just as He did then and will continue to have in the future. The traditions of the past point us to the future, where we will live with Jesus forever. Let the youth decide what traditions they want to establish for Christmas each year and make plans for how they will carry these out. Encourage them to pass on the power of tradition.

CLOSING (5 minutes)

Close with prayer, thanking God for the great gift of the Savior, which we celebrate in this season. Be sure to include any special petitions or prayers of thanks that the students may have mentioned.

THE SAME OLD STORY

CHRISTMAS TRADITIONS

What are some of the things that your family does to celebrate Christmas?

Are there any traditions that started before you were born? If so, what?

Why do families have traditions at Christmas? What is good about traditions?

What would happen if you suddenly couldn't celebrate Christmas the way you had before? What would you do?

What Christmas traditions do you want to pass on to your children?

READING THE STORY

As St. Luke paints a beautiful picture of Christmas, what do you see in the story?

Imagine what the scene looks like. What do Mary and Joseph look like? Where are the shepherds standing? What are the angels singing?

What about this picture do you think gives "peace on earth"?

Why did God send angels to the shepherds and not to the Jewish leaders?

What do Jesus' humble beginnings teach us about God?

What does this account tell you about the purpose of Jesus' ministry?

PASSING ON THE STORY

How did it make you feel when you heard the story read to you again? Do you enjoy hearing it at Christmas? Why?

Why do we keep on celebrating Christmas and reading this old story?

Can you recite the story from memory? Have you ever shared it with anyone?

Since the world has made Christmas so commercial, how can we reach people at Christmastime with God's message of salvation in Jesus?

What can the Christmas story teach us about announcing Christmas today?

What is the real peace Jesus brings at Christmas?

What traditions will this group carry on for next year? Why?

© 2008 Concordia Publishing House. Okay to copy.

37. THE SEARCH IS ON

Luke 2:41–52

Lesson Focus

On our own we are lost in sin, but the Holy Spirit reaches out to us through Word and Sacrament. Our Lord desires us to follow His example in searching the Scriptures, because it is there that we learn about Him and His plan for us.

BEGINNING THE SEARCH (15 minutes)

Distribute copies of the student page, and ask students to tell in which imaginary location they might be found. Ask, "What does your answer tell about your priorities? Are your priorities ones that will help you to grow in wisdom?"

ANXIOUSLY SEARCHING (15 minutes)

Read and discuss Luke 2:41–52. Jesus' parents believed He was traveling with relatives and friends. They didn't understand His priorities, or they would have looked for Him in the temple before three days had passed. Mary and Joseph did not understand Jesus' purpose here on earth. Emphasize that this incident was a misunderstanding, not a sinful act of rebellion by Jesus.

From this story, we learn that Jesus knew the Scriptures well by the time He was twelve. Jesus amazed the people with His knowledge of God's Word. Although He was wiser than His parents, Jesus obeyed them. Have students look at and discuss John 1:1–5, 14. What do these words mean for us? According to 2 Timothy 3:14–17, what benefit is there in studying the Scriptures?

WIDENING THE SEARCH (20 minutes)

Just as Jesus learned from the Scriptures, so do we. Read through the passages together, or, if time is short, assign the verses to individuals.

Romans 5:8—Christ died for us "while we were still sinners."

Acts 2:38—We are to "repent and be baptized" so our sins are forgiven. We will receive the Holy Spirit.

Ephesians 2:8–10—We are saved by grace through faith, not works. But we are created to do good works.

John 5:24— The Word tells us the story of the Savior, in whom we have eternal life.

Philippians 3:20–21—We are citizens of heaven because of Jesus, our Savior. He will transform our lowly bodies so they will be like His glorious body.

As we study God's Word, we grow and mature in our faith and understanding of what God has done for us through the saving work of Christ.

CLOSING (5 minutes)

Thank You, Jesus, for rescuing us when we were lost in our sin. Give us a hunger for Your Word so that we gladly study it and use it as a guide for our lives. Help us to grow in wisdom and desire to do the things You want us to do. We pray in Your name, Jesus. Amen.

LESSON EXTENDERS

✝ What questions might Jesus have asked the teachers in the temple if they were studying Isaiah 40:1–8 or 53:4–10? (Answers will vary.) What might Jesus have taught them about these words? (Jesus may have told them to watch for the fulfillment of these words.) Was Jesus born with all knowledge, or did the Holy Spirit teach it to Him as He studied Scripture? (Though Jesus was true God, as part of His state of humiliation He may not have had the full knowledge available to Him as God. Jesus learned and grew as a normal young person.)

THE SEARCH IS ON

BEGINNING THE SEARCH

If you were separated from your parents while traveling, where would they begin looking for you?

- ❏ Jim's Gigantic Gym
- ❏ Fashion Fads Forever
- ❏ Quick Cuisine Cafe
- ❏ Our Father's Church
- ❏ Arnie's Video Arcade
- ❏ Library R Us
- ❏ Corner of Trouble and Foolishness

What does your answer tell about your parents? What does it tell about you?

ANXIOUSLY SEARCHING

Only one story in the Bible tells us about Jesus as a child. Read it in **Luke 2:41–52**.

What were the three misunderstandings between parents and child?

What do we learn about Jesus from this story?

Read **John 1:1–5, 14** and **2 Timothy 3:14–17**. What significance does God's Word have for us?

What benefit is there to studying the Word?

WIDENING THE SEARCH

Jesus grew in wisdom by studying the Scriptures. As we study the Bible, the Holy Spirit works in our hearts, and we grow in faith and in wisdom. Read the following verses to find basic truths about what God has done for us and how the Scriptures make one "wise for salvation through faith in Christ Jesus" (**2 Timothy 3:15**).

Romans 5:8

Acts 2:38

Ephesians 2:8–10

John 5:24

Philippians 3:20–21

How can these truths help you to grow "in wisdom . . . and in favor with God and men" (**Luke 2:52**)?

© 2008 Concordia Publishing House. Okay to copy.

38. Blessings of Baptism

Mark 1:4–11

Lesson Focus

Students will gain an understanding of John the Baptizer and of Jesus' Baptism and will consider what Baptism means to them.

OPENING (5 minutes)

If possible, obtain the baptismal dates of your students from the church office prior to the lesson. Be sensitive to visitors who may not know their Baptism date or may have been baptized at an older age. Ask students what they know about the day they were baptized. The date? Any family stories about the event? If you were able to obtain baptismal dates, ask students to write their Baptism birth date in their Bibles and/or on the student page.

BAPTIZED UNTO REPENTANCE—JOHN (15 minutes)

Distribute copies of the student page. Ask volunteers to read each passage aloud. As students discuss the questions, share the following information with them:

Jews practiced baptism for Gentiles who converted to Judaism. John's Baptism of Jews was for repentance as God's way of preparing the people for the imminent coming of the Messiah (Malachi 3:1; 4:5–6). John likely lived in the desert region near the Dead Sea or north along the Jordan River. There he baptized people in the Jordan River, which flowed into the Dead Sea about twenty miles from Jerusalem. Compare the idea of people going to the desert with people going on retreat: both are places for people to get away from their daily cares and focus on their spiritual life.

The Holy Spirit leads people in repentance to humble themselves, pray, seek God, turn from wickedness, and forsake evil ways and thoughts. The word *repentance* means to turn around or away from the sinful thought or action and toward faith in Jesus Christ. And God does these things: forgives sin, heals, fully pardons, wipes out sins, and provides refreshment.

John was following in the footsteps of Elijah, wearing animal skins with a leather belt. John's role was to prepare the way for the Messiah.

BAPTIZED FOR US—JESUS (10 minutes)

Discuss this section as a group. Assign passages to various students to read aloud. Help the students understand that the act of Jesus' being baptized is more than just an example for us to follow. (By His Baptism, Jesus gave Himself to the work of "fulfilling all righteousness," showing that God approved Him as the One who would bear the sins of the world.) Through the Holy Spirit, descending on Jesus like a dove, and the voice of God the Father, the Godhead publicly acknowledged Jesus for His work and enabled John truly to testify to Jesus as the Son of God.

BAPTIZED—WE LIVE (25 minutes)

Divide the passage among students. After about five minutes, ask those with the same passage to read that passage aloud and share their findings. Provide large sheets of paper, magazines, scissors, and glue. Direct the students to create a group collage with pictures that depict the benefits of Baptism: salvation, forgiveness of sins, the indwelling of the Holy Spirit, a new life in Christ, being united with Christ at the resurrection, and being clothed with Christ. Hang the collage in your classroom or meeting area.

Close with a prayer of thanks for the benefits of Baptism.

LESSON EXTENDERS

✝ Use the explanation section of Luther's Small Catechism to look in-depth at these topics:

Repentance (see The Office of the Keys, Questions 269–77)

The Blessings of Baptism (Questions 248–52)

Blessings of Baptism

BAPTIZED UNTO REPENTANCE—JOHN

Read **Mark 1:4–6**.

What do you know about Jewish beliefs regarding baptism?

Why would John want the people to come out of Jerusalem to the desert?

Read **2 Chronicles 7:14**; **Isaiah 55:7**; and **Acts 3:19**. List words that describe the human actions involved in repentance. List words that describe God's response to repentance.

Compare **Mark 1:6** with **2 Kings 1:7–9**. What do you discover about a prophet's wardrobe?

Read **Mark 1:2–3, 7–8**. How would you describe John's purpose in life?

BAPTIZED FOR US—JESUS

Read **Mark 1:9–11**.

Why did Jesus, who had no need of repentance, come to John to be baptized? **Matthew 3:15** may shed some light on the subject.

What do you think the dove and voice meant to Jesus? to John? Read **John 1:32–34**. How did this event enable John to better fulfill his purpose in life?

BAPTIZED—WE LIVE

Read the passages below to discover the benefits of your own Baptism.

Mark 16:16

Acts 2:38–39

Romans 6:3–5

Galatians 3:27

© 2008 Concordia Publishing House. Okay to copy.

39. Beyond Miracles

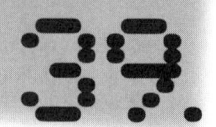

John 2:1–11

Lesson Focus

Although the world looks to new miracles and the latest supernatural discoveries for a spiritual experience, we find our salvation in the miraculous love and sacrifice of Jesus on the cross.

MIRACLES DEFINED
(5 minutes)

Distribute copies of the student page, and give students time to reflect on miracles. Where have they heard about miracles? What movies have they seen that portray miracles? (Perhaps movie classics like *It's a Wonderful Life, The Bishop's Wife, Miracle on 34th Street, The Preacher's Wife,* or others.) Encourage students to describe miracles portrayed in movies and television; later these will be compared with the biblical model.

JESUS' MIRACLES
(30 minutes)

Discuss the reading of John 2:1–11 and the miracle Jesus performed. Consider what He meant by saying, "My time has not yet come" (v. 4).

The miracles of Jesus show us that He has authority over creation and the devil. Divide the class into pairs or read the suggested passages as a group to determine what it is that Jesus shows His authority over as He performs these miracles. (The miracles performed show Jesus' authority over demons, sicknesses, and death, but in Luke 5:17–26, Jesus also shows authority over sin.)

Next, have students read John 2:11. Discuss the result of the miracles, which is to reveal Christ's glory and to help the disciples believe. Why would Jesus need to help His disciples believe?

Then, read John 20:29. Discuss Thomas's reluctance to believe without seeing the scars of Jesus. How is this reluctance to believe like searching for proof in miracles or the supernatural?

Discuss the miracle of Christ's redemption for us. We sin; He forgives. We deserve death; He dies in our place. The real miracle of the Christian faith is that Jesus loved us so much that He died to save us from our sins. Both Jesus' resurrection and His death on the cross were miraculous.

THE MIRACLE OF FAITH
(10 minutes)

Encourage students to read and answer the questions for each verse, leading to the last question of this section. God creates the miracle of faith in each believer as the Holy Spirit works through the Word of God, Baptism, and the Lord's Supper. Consider reviewing the explanation of the Third Article of the Creed in Luther's Small Catechism for the class.

MIRACLES—BIBLE-STYLE (5 minutes)

Finally, return to your discussion of popular culture's view of miracles. How are Jesus' miracles different from the ones you discussed? The best miracle of all is the love of God for us in Jesus. Close in prayer, thanking God for His miraculous gift of faith.

LESSON EXTENDERS

✝ Have students work together to make a group poster or mural with the statement at the top "Celebrate the Miracle of God's Love." Encourage them to create pictures of Bible stories, including scenes of the death and resurrection of Jesus. They could also sketch pictures of other "miracles": Baptism, Communion, or a picture of a Bible.

✝ See how a songwriter tells the story of Thomas; review "O Sons and Daughters of the King" (*LSB* 470/471; *LW* 130).

Beyond Miracles

MIRACLES DEFINED
What do you think of when you hear the word *miracle*?

What are some examples of miracles (from the Bible or from everyday life)?

What miracles are portrayed in movies or television shows?

JESUS' MIRACLES
Read **John 2:1–11**. What miracle did Jesus perform?

What are some other miracles Jesus performed? What do these passages show that Jesus has authority over (for example, sickness, devil, death)?

Luke 4:31–37

Luke 4:38–44

Luke 5:12–16

Luke 9:37–45

John 11:38–43

Luke 5:17–26

What happens as a result of miracles? (See **John 2:11**.)

THE MIRACLE OF FAITH
Read these verses, and then answer the questions below:

Romans 10:17—Where does faith come from?

John 3:5–6—How does a person enter the kingdom of God?

1 Peter 1:23—What creates your new birth (becoming born again)?

Thinking of these verses and the answers to the questions, tell how God creates the miracle of faith in you.

MIRACLES—BIBLE-STYLE
How is popular culture's view of miracles different from the Bible?

What is the best miracle? (See **Ephesians 2:4–6**.)

© 2008 Concordia Publishing House. Okay to copy.

STUDENT PAGE 39

40. You Have the Right Not to Remain Silent

John 1:29–41; Matthew 9:9–13

Lesson Focus

Young people receive God's power and purpose as they share God's amazing and saving grace in Christ Jesus.

INTRODUCTION (5 minutes)

When police make arrests, they are required to advise the people being taken into custody of their rights. These are called Miranda rights. They protect the rights of the alleged criminals. Ask students to recite any of the Miranda rights that they know. Be sure that they cite the phrase "you have the right to remain silent."

Being silent about our faith is not *a* right, nor is it *right*. Rather, as redeemed sinners, saved by God's grace in Christ, we are witnesses. The Holy Spirit places in our minds and mouths the words to say. Even our lives can declare the impact of what God has done. In thoughts, deeds, and words, we tell the world who Jesus Christ is, what He did on Calvary, and what He does through Word and Sacrament ministry.

HOW'S YOUR TALK? (20 minutes)

Distribute copies of the student page. Have one student read John 1:29–41. Allow time for students to answer and discuss the questions from the student page. What are some of the ways we can speak publicly about our faith in Jesus as our personal Savior and Lord?

Jesus as . . .
- the sin away-taker (John 1:29)
- the way-maker (John 14:6)
- the bondage breaker (Ezra 9:9a)

John speaks . . .
- publicly
- straightforwardly
- strongly, unabashedly
- using an image of a lamb to relate the way the Jews understood sacrifice for sin
- by starting with what was familiar to the Jewish faith

Any person who follows Jesus is responding to God's work through the Holy Spirit. Andrew heard John's testimony about Jesus—faith comes from hearing the message of the Gospel (Romans 10:17). Andrew may have heard others talk about their faith. God leads Andrew to jump into action in verse 41—he can't remain silent. When Andrew speaks the truth, the Holy Spirit works change in Peter's life.

OTHERS WHO HEARD THE GOOD NEWS (20 minutes)

Have students read the selected verses and answer the questions from the student page. Matthew wrote this Gospel, which shares the message of salvation through Christ. Discuss students' insights.

Have students consider the wise implications of 1 Corinthians 15:33. Teachers may want to remind students that when they regularly participate in Holy Communion, they are publicly professing that they believe what the church teaches. The Eucharist is an intensely sacred activity—and more, instituted by Christ, with the promise of forgiveness in Christ. It is much more than simply eating with your sisters and brothers in faith. Jesus is the host, as God's Word through the pastor's words reminds us of the real presence of Christ in, with, and under bread and wine, His body and His blood.

CLOSING (5 minutes)

Close with a group prayer, thanking God for His gift of forgiveness through His body and blood. Be sure to include any special prayer requests from the students.

LESSON EXTENDERS

✝ John the Baptizer calls out in John 1:29 and 36, "Look, the Lamb of God!" From that day down by the riverside to the day of his death, John gave witness to Jesus as the light (John 1:7). John gave his life as a witness. The word *martyr* comes from the Greek word meaning "witness." John lost his head because of his faith in Jesus (Matthew 14:1–12). Discuss some of the sacrifices made for Christ's sake today.

You Have the Right Not to Remain Silent

HOW'S YOUR TALK?

Read **John 1:29–41**.

What are some phrases these verses use to describe what Jesus has done as our personal Savior and Lord (**John 1:29; John 14:6; Ezra 9:9a**)?

What characterizes the way John the Baptizer talks about Jesus?

What motivates Andrew (Peter's brother) to follow Jesus, **verse 40**?

OTHERS WHO HEARD THE GOOD NEWS

Read **Matthew 9:9–13**.

How did this person share the Good News that first changed him?

What do your friends and the people you hang out with **tell** others about what you believe (see **1 Corinthians 15:33**)?

How does God help you resist negative influences in your life?

Whom do you know who really needs to hear the Gospel of Jesus Christ?

What can you do with God's help?

© 2008 Concordia Publishing House. Okay to copy.

STUDENT PAGE 40

41. WHICH IS EASIER?

Mark 2:1–12

Lesson Focus

Through His death and resurrection, Jesus does what we could not do for ourselves—He restores us to a healthy relationship with God.

WHICH IS EASIER?
(15 minutes)

For this activity, you may want to have students form groups based on their answer to the situation below. For example, all those who think waking up at 5:00 a.m. is easier would get up and form a group (the 5:00 p.m. people would do the same). Then give each group a chance to support/defend its choice.

Which is easier?
—Waking up at 5:00 a.m. or going to sleep at 5:00 p.m.?
—Having a cold or having the flu?
—A guy asking a girl out or a girl asking a guy out?

A LOOK AT SCRIPTURE
(15 minutes)

Distribute copies of the student page. Read Mark 2:1–12. Many sick and disabled people found access to Jesus for healing. On the basis of his friends' actions, what could have been the condition of the paralytic on a scale of 1 (moderate) to 10 (desperate)? (Answers will vary.) What elements of friendship are exhibited by the paralytic's friends? (Answers will vary but might include faith in Christ, determination, loyalty, work, and sacrifice.) Which is easier, forgiving sins or healing the body? (Both are equally easy for God and equally impossible for humankind.)

A LOOK IN THE MIRROR
(20 minutes)

Have students work in pairs to answer the questions in this section. Then review with the whole group. This story from the Gospel of Mark mirrors our relationship with God. How are we like the paralytic? (We are paralyzed with sin from our own destructive choices.) Another mark of friendship is doing something for someone that he or she could not do. What does Jesus do for us that we can't do for ourselves? (Removes the barrier of sin so that we might be in fellowship with God) What elements of friendship does Jesus exhibit? (Answers will vary.) How are we healed? (With forgiveness earned by Christ, new life through our Baptism, eternal life) Why are we healed? (So that we may be His own and live under Him in His kingdom, that we might know the length and width and height and depth of the love of God)

CLOSING (5 minutes)

Close with prayer: "Heavenly Father, You are our great healer. You've forgiven us and healed our brokenness. Fill us with Your Spirit so we might share Your healing with those we meet. Through Jesus Christ, Your Son. Amen."

LESSON EXTENDERS

✝ Memory-work twist: Grab a sign-language dictionary from the library, and demonstrate the signs for the key words of 2 Corinthians 3:18.

WHICH IS EASIER?

A LOOK AT SCRIPTURE

Read **Mark 2:1–12**.

On the basis of his friends' actions, what could have been the condition of the paralytic on a scale of 1 (moderate) to 10 (desperate)?

What elements of friendship are exhibited by the paralytic's friends?

Which is easier, forgiving sins or healing the body?

A LOOK IN THE MIRROR

This story from the Gospel of Mark mirrors our relationship with God. How are we like the paralytic? What does Jesus do for us that we can't do for ourselves?

What elements of friendship does Jesus exhibit?

How are we healed? (See **Romans 6:3–7**.)

Why are we healed? (See **Romans 8:39**.)

42. JESUS, MY LIGHT

John 9

Lesson Focus

Without Christ, people live in darkness. Christ is the light of the world who brings sight to the blind.

BLINDNESS (5 minutes)

Ask, "What would it be like to be physically blind? What does it mean to be spiritually blind?" Allow students to reflect and share responses.

LIVING IN THE DARK (15 minutes)

Distribute copies of the student page. Divide the passages among pairs of students. Ask students to read their passage and be prepared to share what it reveals about the Pharisees' blindness. Possible responses: John 9:15–17—The spiritual leaders ask the blind beggar for his opinion. John 9:18–19—They wouldn't believe him, so they sent for his parents. John 9:24—Speaking with the blind beggar again, they stated that they know "this man" (Jesus) is a sinner. John 9:28–29—They claim to be Moses' disciples; they don't know where "this fellow" (Jesus) comes from. John 9:34—They get angry with the healed beggar and are unwilling to hear something other than what they want to hear. John 9:39–40—They do not understand their own predicament.

Ask students to read the rest of the questions in this section. Call on volunteers to share responses. Accept all responses. Help students understand that some people have made up their minds not to believe in Jesus and are unwilling to consider any alternative. Many scientists and people who consider themselves atheists or agnostics have this attitude.

LIVING IN THE LIGHT (15 minutes)

Divide the passages among students. Ask students to read their passage and be prepared to share what it indicates about the blind beggar's understanding of Jesus. Possible responses: John 9:7—The man obeys Jesus. John 9:11–12—He tells only the facts of his healing. John 9:17b—He considers Jesus a prophet. John 9:24–25—He is certain enough of Jesus to contradict the Pharisees (an action sure to get him thrown out of the synagogue). John 9:27—He implies that he is a disciple of Jesus. John 9:30–33—He contradicts and lectures the Pharisees. He implies that Jesus must be from God. John 9:35–38—He expresses his belief in Jesus as the Son of Man (i.e., the Messiah), and he worships Jesus, an act that a Jew reserves for God alone.

Ask students to consider the remaining questions. Solicit volunteers to share responses. Accept all answers. Guide students to see that growth of the man's spiritual understanding began when Jesus touched him and he was strengthened by the Holy Spirit. These circumstances caused him to think more deeply about Jesus. Jesus does not leave the man with a shallow understanding, but returns to provide the man with full sight of Himself.

JESUS THE LIGHT (10 minutes)

Read the passages aloud together. Ask for volunteers to respond to both questions. Guide students to understand that God has provided the Bible, Baptism, and Communion as means of seeing Jesus. Christians also share the light of Christ with others.

MY SIGHT (10 minutes)

Allow students to quietly read the questions and be prepared to share responses. Make sure that students understand that true growth comes only through God. We grow in our faith as we hear His Word and partake of the Sacraments. Close with prayer.

Jesus, My Light

LIVING IN THE DARK
Read the following passages from the Book of John, and consider how they reveal the Pharisees' blindness.

John 9:15–17

John 9:18–19

John 9:24

John 9:28–29

John 9:34

John 9:39–40

What hinders the Pharisees' spiritual sight? How would you describe their character? What types of people today are like the Pharisees?

LIVING IN THE LIGHT
What do the following verses indicate about the blind beggar's growth in sight?

John 9:7

John 9:11–12

John 9:17b

John 9:24–25

John 9:27

John 9:30–33

John 9:35–38

What circumstances caused the beggar's spiritual sight to increase? In what ways could the blind man agree with the words of the hymn "Amazing Grace"—"I once was lost but now am found, Was blind but now I see"?

JESUS THE LIGHT
John portrays Jesus as light more than any other Gospel writer. How does this story illustrate Jesus' words in **John 8:12**; **9:5**; and **12:44–46**? What does it mean to you?

MY SIGHT
In what ways has your spiritual sight grown lately?

How do people gain sight of Jesus today?

When has God used you to help someone else see Jesus? Did the person respond more like the blind beggar or like the Pharisees?

43. You're in Good Company!

Mark 6:1–13

Lesson Focus

People were offended by Jesus when they saw only His humanity and not His divinity. We tell others of Jesus' love and trust His promise to be with us—even though some may be offended!

OPENING (5 minutes)

Ask your students, "If your brother or sister became famous and everybody was oohing and aahing over him or her, how might you feel? Your response might be 'Gag!' or 'Big deal!' " Ask, "Why would you feel that way?" (They grew up knowing him or her, including weaknesses and bad habits.) Then ask, "What if your brother was Jesus—how might things be different?" (Check for responses.) "Today we will see what our Savior endured for us and how, when we suffer for His name, we are in His good company!"

GETTING INTO SCRIPTURE (15 minutes)

Distribute copies of the student page. Have students read Mark 6:1–3. Invite the students to thumb through the previous chapters of Mark and think about all that Jesus taught—backed up by so many miracles. His neighbors and extended family did not believe that He was special because they knew His family so well. They took offense at the thought of "their Jesus" being God.

GOING DEEPER (15 minutes)

Read Mark 6:4–6a. By declaring that "Only in his hometown . . . is a prophet without honor," Jesus included Himself in the line of God's prophets who lived before Him. Though privileged to watch Jesus grow up, the people in Jesus' hometown refused to believe He was their Savior. Because of their unbelief, Jesus did not perform miracles as He did in other places to strengthen people's faith. Our Lord never performed a "magic show" to convince unbelievers who He was. Therefore, He chose not to perform miracles in His hometown. The instructions Jesus gave His disciples in 6:6b–13 explained God's power and gave a preview of their mission work—where they would see others receive and reject Christ.

PONDERING THE GOSPEL (15 minutes)

Read the student page comments and invite responses.

Clearly, the crucifixion of our Lord was the ultimate picture of someone in the middle of bad company, with jeering crowds and criminals nailed on either side. The real bad company included the multitude of our sins, which surrounded Him on the cross. Thank God that Jesus stayed on the cross so all of our sins would be taken away forever!

As those first disciples soon discovered, bearing the name *Christian* invites harsh treatment in a sinful world. We can rejoice and be glad because our real home is in heaven in the company of Christ! Invite students to share about and offer encouragement to each other for times they felt under attack for being in Jesus' "good company."

CLOSING (5 minutes)

In your closing prayer, reflect the experiences the students shared, asking God for strength to boldly let the world know we belong to Jesus. Conclude with the Lord's Prayer.

LESSON EXTENDERS

✝ See 2 Corinthians 11:24–31. When we suffer harassment for bearing Jesus' name, consider the apostle Paul's sufferings!

✝ See Hebrews 11:32–12:3. Surrounded by such great company, on whom do we now also keep our eyes focused, as did our brothers and sisters of ancient times?

You're in Good Company!

GETTING INTO SCRIPTURE

Read **Mark 6:1–3**. By this time, Jesus had become famous for the message He proclaimed and the miracles He performed. When Jesus arrived back home, how did people regard Jesus . . . concerning His past career?

concerning His family members?

What was the result of them remembering His past in that town and not understanding His ministry among them?

GOING DEEPER

Read **Mark 6:4–6a**. Normally, a reunion of family and neighbors can be a good time. What did Jesus have to say about how reunions could be for prophets?

What impact did the people's reaction to Jesus have on His ministry among them?

Why do you suppose that was so?

Read **Mark 6:6b–13**. In light of what our Savior endured from unbelievers, what instructions did He give His disciples?

PONDERING THE GOSPEL

Share your reflections on the thoughts below.

To think of Jesus as God offended these hometown folks. See **Mark 15:25–32**. After Jesus was rejected, where did He serve?

See **Matthew 5:11–12**. When people are mean to those who love Jesus, how can we "rejoice and be glad"? In whose company are we then included?

Can you think of any times that you felt under attack (small or great) for being in the "good company" of Jesus?

© 2008 Concordia Publishing House. Okay to copy.

44. A Familiar Voice

John 10:1–18

Lesson Focus

Young people hear many false voices. Our Good Shepherd Jesus knows, loves, leads, and protects us and calls us by name. By God's grace we can recognize and listen to Jesus' voice.

OPENING (5 minutes)

Blindfold a volunteer. Have other students stand behind the volunteer and speak, at first softly or in disguised voices, then louder and in normal tones. See if the volunteer can identify the voices. Let others volunteer.

FALSE MESSAGES (5 minutes)

Distribute copies of the student page. Read the opening paragraph and question. Misleading voices could include "Abortion is only getting rid of a fetus," "Using drugs won't really hurt you," "Violence is the best way," "Sex before marriage is acceptable," or "Other people can be used and manipulated."

THE SHEPHERD'S VOICE (20 minutes)

Have the students work in pairs or small groups, reading John 10:1–15 and 1 John 4:1–6 and discussing the questions on the student page. (If you have a large group or a short amount of time, assign one passage to each half of the class.) Invite the groups to report their responses. Incorporate the following as you discuss the answers:

(1) Distracting voices are all around us. The student page mentions some. Others might include friends or teachers who are not Christians, advertising, or movies. Press for specific examples from the students' lives. Point out that Satan, the father of lies (John 8:44), is sly in getting us to follow wrong voices.

(2) Jesus gave up His life for us, His sheep. Through constant loving care, He has trained us to hear His voice. Again seek specific examples from the students' lives.

(3) The anti-Christian voices of the world are easy to recognize—if we know the "Spirit of truth." Bank tellers learn to identify counterfeit money by training for hours using *real* currency. They become so familiar with the real item that a false bill is immediately identifiable. Christians spend time getting to know our Savior through His Word. Then we can recognize error.

(4) The worldly voices around us were overcome when we were buried with Christ in Baptism and raised to new life through faith in Him. Every time we recall that Jesus died for our sins, we are strengthened to follow Him.

LISTEN AND FOLLOW (20 minutes)

Invite the students to respond to the case studies. Ask them to "listen to Jesus," remembering the encouragement He provides through His Word and imagining what He would say in that situation. Also ask what *they* might say to those who tempt them in those ways.

CLOSING (5 minutes)

Remind the students that Jesus knows us by name. He knows us better than anyone else can. He goes before us, leading the way—a good way. He desires such a close relationship with us that when a strange voice tries to lead us in a false way we will recognize the imposter and run away. Close with a prayer of thanks for His strength.

LESSON EXTENDERS

✝ Search newspapers or magazines for worldly voices that contradict God's Word and for examples of people responding to Jesus' voice. Pray for these real-life situations.

✝ Brainstorm a list of "voices of the Gospel" that can be heard in your community (such as church services and sermons, Bible study opportunities, and Christian radio and television programs).

A Familiar Voice

FALSE MESSAGES

It can be difficult living in a society that sends conflicting messages to us constantly. Every time we watch television or videos, listen to music on the radio, or read a magazine, we may hear messages that are contrary to God's plan for our lives. What are some of the false messages you have heard?

THE SHEPHERD'S VOICE

Read **John 10:1–15**.

1. What "voices" in our world try to distract us from listening to Christ's voice? Who is speaking?

2. Why can we trust Jesus' voice? How do we come to know Jesus' voice?

Read **1 John 4:4–6**.

3. How can we recognize "the spirit of falsehood"—those who speak from the world's point of view?

4. John says we have already overcome the false voices of the world. When did that happen? How can it help us now?

LISTEN AND FOLLOW

Your friend Lexi comes to you and tells you how her boyfriend wants her to skip the chaperoned after-prom party and go to his friend's house, where the parents are out of town.

Ryan comes to you and tells you that he plans to get some steroids that will help him "beef up" and give him a chance of becoming a starter next year on the football team. Do you want in?

You and your friend Li want to go to a movie. Between the two of you, you only have enough money for one ticket. Li knows where his sister keeps her babysitting money and plans to "borrow" it.

© 2008 Concordia Publishing House. Okay to copy.

STUDENT PAGE 44

45. Resting in Jesus

Luke 10:38–42;
Matthew 11:28

Lesson Focus

Some teens are driven to do many things for God. Jesus has done all that the Law requires of us and invites us to rest in Him, rather than strive by our own efforts to please Him.

OPENING (5 minutes)

Ask the students, "How much sleep do you get at night?" Wait for responses. Ask, "Do you ever take a nap to get extra sleep? If you do, how long do you sleep?"

THE NEED FOR REST (15 minutes)

Distribute copies of the student page. Allow time for the students to answer the questions about the need for rest. Invite volunteers to share their answers. Also invite them to share an example when their performance dropped or relationships were hurt by their being tired.

Then ask whether most people work too much or rest too much. Ask students to explain their choice. Then ask, "What does faith in Jesus have to do with rest?"

REST IN THE WORD (20 minutes)

Ask students to follow along as you read aloud Luke 10:38–42. Read the quotes dramatically, as they might have been uttered. Allow the students to work in pairs to answer the questions from the student page. Have each pair share their answers with the group.

Read Matthew 11:28–30 aloud. Share how the Law is a heavy burden that makes us weary. You might want to share the cliché "There is no rest for the wicked." Trying to follow the Law for our salvation will not provide rest; we will always fail. What does Jesus promise to give to those who come to Him?

REST IN JESUS (5 minutes)

Discuss when and how normal Christian activities, such as prayer, worship, witnessing, Bible study, and service, can become burdens that distract us from Jesus.

Ask the students to share their preferred definition of *rest* from the choices on the student page. Ask the students to tell what it means to rest in Jesus.

CLOSING (5 minutes)

Pray aloud the following, pausing for students to silently pray: "Dear Father, forgive us when we, like Martha, get distracted and focus on our works for You. We list those areas now where we try to impress You. (pause) Spirit, remind us that Jesus has done all that's necessary for our salvation and nothing we can do will make us more pleasing in the Father's eyes. (pause) Jesus, we thank and praise You for obeying the Father, dying for us, and promising eternal rest with You someday. May we always rest in You and in what You have done for us. In Your precious name. Amen."

LESSON EXTENDERS

✝ Psalm 62:1 reads, "My soul finds rest in God alone." Ask the students where people try to find rest apart from God.

✝ Ask the students to discuss how they and their families spend Sundays. Is it really restful? What could make it more restful?

Resting in Jesus

THE NEED FOR REST
Why do you think God created a day for rest?

What happens when you are tired and need rest?

How do you feel?

How well do you perform activities?

How well do you relate to others, such as family and friends?

REST IN THE WORD
Read **Luke 10:38–42**. Describe how Martha must have felt.

When and where have you felt that way?

Verse 40 says Martha was "distracted." *Distracted* means "drawn away." Where should Martha have given her attention? What things led Martha to be "worried and upset"?

REST IN JESUS
Rest is

1. refreshing ease;

2. relief or freedom from anxiety; and

3. to have tranquility or peace.

Which definition of *rest* do you prefer? Why?

What does it mean to "rest in Jesus"?

© 2008 Concordia Publishing House. Okay to copy.

STUDENT PAGE 45

46. Strengthened by His Glory

Matthew 17:1–9

Lesson Focus

God still reveals His glory to young people today in order to strengthen their faith, comfort them, and embolden them for witness.

WHY DON'T I FEEL STRONG IN MY FAITH? (10 minutes)

Distribute copies of the student page. Cut out five to ten articles from yesterday's paper, or use the headlines listed on the student page. Have students choose the articles that might encourage their security. Have them list the articles that discourage their faith. Have them list the articles that are neutral. Discuss how many sources in our daily lives discourage us in our faith versus how many sources encourage us. Because we live in a fallen world, there are a multitude of sources of discouragement to our faith in Jesus. News can't increase our hope or joy—only the Good News of Jesus Christ is truly able to encourage us. (You can point out that because of sin, most human behavior is discouraging, less than glorious, and even shameful, "for all have sinned and fall short of the glory of God" [Romans 3:23].) How can faith in Jesus be encouraged if the predominant behavior of human beings is so discouraging, so shameful, and so far short of God's glorious ways?

TOUCHED BY HIS GLORY (30 minutes)

Ask the students to share with each other (in groups of two or three) their own sources of encouragement in their faith in Jesus. What activities, people, or circumstances have built up their faith in Jesus? Be prepared to share a Bible story, real-life situation, or Bible passage that encourages faith in youth.

Read the Bible passages and discuss the questions. Suggested responses:

Some examples might include watching people who stand up for truth in the face of opposition, a parent who brings you to church and prays with you, and a pastor's funeral sermon speaking about seeing a loved one again in heaven because Jesus paid for that person's sins.

Examples might be Christians who don't act like they ought, racism, selfishness, and immorality.

Descriptions might include awesome, totally pure, too wonderful to describe, and so on.

Jesus revealed His glory to let His disciples see Him as He truly is so that they may know the truth and then declare it to others.

Moses was frightened and later emboldened by God's glory.

The Israelites were fearful of God's glory.

The disciples described their hearts burning within them.

They realized their own sinfulness and smallness and yet were strengthened to serve God.

God's glory comes to everyone in the Word of God and the Sacraments. His glory is especially seen through the conversion of sinners to Christ.

CLOSING (10 minutes)

Sitting in circles of two or three people, pray together for God to reveal His glory more and more to each individual and to use each individual to shine God's glory into others' lives, especially His glorious forgiveness and mercy.

LESSON EXTENDERS

✝ Read 2 Corinthians 3:7–11. What is more glorious, the proclamation of the Law or the proclamation of the Gospel? What scriptural instances do you recall with the angels' singing (rejoicing) in heaven? (At the birth of the Savior, when one sinner repents, etc.)

Strengthened by His Glory

WHY DON'T I FEEL STRONG IN MY FAITH?

Place a check next to the headlines that encourage the security of your faith in Jesus; place an X next to those that discourage it.

____ "Homeless Man Found Dead"

____ "Teen Pregnancy Numbers on the Rise"

____ "Mrs. Charlene O'Bannon Elected First Female Mayor"

____ "Campaign Funding Again Investigated by State Attorney General"

____ "Boy Scouts File Lawsuit against ACLU in Gay Scout Leader Case"

____ "Mighty Monarchs Bring Home Regional Second-Place Trophy"

____ "Hubble Telescope Records Dramatic Pictures of Forming Solar Systems"

____ "Local Churches Squabble over Parking Lot and Property Lines"

____ "Recycling Plant 'A Necessity,' the Governor Says"

TOUCHED BY HIS GLORY

What activities, people, or circumstances have built up your faith in Jesus?

What less-than-glorious behavior weakens or discourages your faith in Jesus?

How would you describe the glory of the Lord?

Read **Matthew 17:1–9**. For what purpose(s) did Jesus reveal His glory to Peter, James, and John?

Read **Exodus 3:4–6, 11–12**. How did Moses react to the glory of the Lord?

Read **Exodus 20:18–19**. How did the people of Israel react to God's glory?

Read **Luke 24:13–35**. How did the two disciples describe how they felt while listening to the risen Lord Jesus during their walk to Emmaus?

How were Moses, the people of Israel, and the two disciples changed by their encounters with glory?

Where and when can believers (and nonbelievers) encounter the glory of the Lord today?

© 2008 Concordia Publishing House. Okay to copy.

47. Fellowship with the Lamb

Luke 22:7–38

Lesson Focus

Because of the sacrifice of the Lamb, we are able to share in fellowship with Christ and each other through Communion, and we will share in the feast of fellowship with Him eternally!

What's on the Menu? (15 minutes)

Discuss the festivities and traditions that go along with family celebrations. As you look at the Scripture and questions about the Passover, connect the concepts of tradition and commemoration. Jesus told His disciples exactly what to do and what they would find. Everything was just as He said. This way of preparation was a witness to the omniscience of Christ and of His loving care for His disciples.

Lessons from the Past, Lessons of That Day (15 minutes)

Allow students to work in breakout groups to discuss the questions in this section. Emphasize the following: The Passover was a commanded celebration of the Israelites' deliverance from the angel of death that passed over Egypt. The blood of a sacrificed lamb was used to mark the doors.

Christ was also preparing for the sacrifice of Himself. His sacrifice would deliver us, His people, from the captivity and ultimate death of sin. (You may wish to point out the parallels between Christ and the Passover lamb.)

Have students look at Hebrews 10:1–14 and answer the question. Emphasize the "once and for all" nature of Christ's sacrifice (v. 10).

Christ in Fellowship with His Disciples—And Us (10 minutes)

Christ institutes the Lord's Supper, or Holy Communion. Through Communion we share in fellowship with Christ and with each other.

We also join with those who have gone before us. Remind the class that each week before we commune, we hear the words "Therefore with angels and archangels and with all the company of heaven we laud and magnify Your glorious name, evermore praising You and saying . . . " We are joined not just with the believers here and now, but with the whole company of heaven—all those who have gone before us. Allow students to discuss this point first, although they may need some guidance in reaching the intended conclusion.

Looking to the Future (10 minutes)

Jesus says, "I will not eat it again until it finds fulfillment in the kingdom of God" (Luke 22:16). The Passover will be fulfilled at the wedding supper of the Lamb, when Christ comes again and we will be in fellowship with Him forever.

Jesus knew that in His suffering and death He was to be the Passover sacrifice to atone for our sins and deliver us from death. In this Passover meal, Christ was sharing in fellowship with His disciples. Through His institution of the Lord's Supper, He provides a way for us, His disciples, to remain in fellowship with Him until He comes again in the ultimate fulfillment of the Passover. The Lamb will then come in glory to deliver His people eternally and to be in fellowship with them at the wedding supper of the Lamb.

Closing (5 minutes)

Pray a prayer of thanksgiving for Christ's atoning sacrifice for our sake. Ask that He would keep our hearts in fellowship with Him now and for all eternity.

Fellowship with the Lamb

WHAT'S ON THE MENU?

What is the biggest and best celebration meal of the year for your family? What foods do you normally eat? Are there special activities that go along with the day? What is your favorite part of the celebration?

Read **Luke 22:7–38**. What was unusual about how the disciples prepared for the Passover meal?

How was this a witness to them of the lordship of Christ?

LESSONS FROM THE PAST, LESSONS OF THAT DAY

What was the significance of the Passover to the Jewish people? (**Exodus 12**, especially **v. 17**)

At the Passover, it was the blood of what kind of animal that was used to mark the doors of the houses and deliver the people inside from death? (**Exodus 12:3–7**)

In addition to the Passover lamb, for what sacrifice was Christ preparing? (**Luke 22:15**)

What would this sacrifice accomplish?

Look at **Hebrews 10:1–14**, and discuss the difference in Christ's sacrifice.

CHRIST IN FELLOWSHIP WITH HIS DISCIPLES—AND US

Luke 22:15 indicates Christ's desire to share in the fellowship of the Passover meal with His disciples. What Sacrament does Christ then institute? (**vv. 17–20**)

In addition to the forgiveness of sins, what does our celebration of Communion allow us to have?

LOOKING TO THE FUTURE

In **verse 16**, Jesus says He will not eat the Passover again until when?

When will that be? (Read **Revelation 19:9**.)

A fellowship celebration with Christ that lasts forever—now that's something to look forward to!

© 2008 Concordia Publishing House. Okay to copy.

STUDENT PAGE 47

48. GODFORSAKEN?!

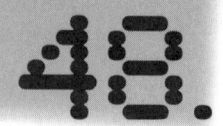

Mark 15:21–47

Lesson Focus

While on the cross Jesus was forsaken by His Father so that we might forsake all earthly things for the Father's sake.

OPENING (15 minutes)

Invite the class to play a survivor-style game called "Abandon Ship!" Have students form a lifeboat by putting chairs into a circle, after first choosing a captain. Hand out paper for a secret ballot to elect the most likely candidate. When the captain is chosen, inform him or her that since the captain's job is to go down with the ship, he or she is excluded from the lifeboat and must face a corner of the room for the remainder of the game. Re-form the life raft by encircling chairs, but make sure there is one fewer chair than students, forcing someone to stand in the middle. Have the students elect a new captain, again by secret ballot, then instruct that person that they must serve the crew by jumping overboard and drowning (facing a different corner), since there is not enough space in the raft. Elect a third captain by secret ballot, then inform the new captain that there is not enough food for everyone, and have that person ask for one or two volunteers to jump overboard (to a third and fourth corner). Finally, instruct the remaining students that they have been rescued, and give them a small reward for being survivors—perhaps Life Savers or a similar treat.

Gather the entire class and interview those who didn't survive. Ask: How did it feel to not be a survivor with the rest of the group? Was it better to be elected or to volunteer? Was it worth being forsaken to save the class?

THE AWFUL TRUTH (10 minutes)

Distribute copies of the student page. Have students take turns reading St. Mark's crucifixion account. Discuss the questions with the class. Help the students to recognize the agony Christ must have felt being forsaken by His Father after the intimacy of their fellowship. Discuss the necessity of such punishment. Jesus' sacrifice gave believers victory over sin and eternal death, which would not have happened if God the Father had rescued His Son on the cross. Point out any parallels to the opening activity. God had created the salvation plan and bound Himself to it.

THE AWESOME TRIUMPH (10 minutes)

Encourage breakout groups to brainstorm this section. After about seven minutes, have volunteers share their ideas with the class. Be sure to point out that people often blame God when they feel abandoned, yet we know from Scripture that God is near the brokenhearted.

THE AWKWARD TIMES (10 minutes)

Let the students reflect and work on this section by themselves, but encourage them to share their work with at least one other person if they finish before the class.

CLOSING (5 minutes)

Invite the students to read their psalms aloud if they are willing. If not, read Psalm 94:14–19 together. Then close with a prayer thanking God for His promise to never forsake us and asking His strength for times we feel abandoned.

LESSON EXTENDERS

✝ Read Acts 2:25–31, part of Peter's sermon on Pentecost. How does Christ's resurrection assure us, as it did David, that God will never abandon us? Who seems most forsaken in our neighborhoods? How can we show them God's loving and eternal presence?

GODFORSAKEN?!

THE AWFUL TRUTH

Read **Mark 15:21–47**. To *forsake* means to abandon and renounce someone who had been dear to you.

Why was it so agonizing for Jesus to be forsaken by His Father?

How would the story be different if God had not forsaken Jesus?

Why would God have to forsake us if He had not forsaken Jesus?

THE AWESOME TRIUMPH

God's Word and the gifts of Baptism and Communion assure us that, because God abandoned Jesus on the cross, He will never abandon us. God has said, "'Never will I leave you; never will I forsake you.' So we say with confidence, 'The Lord is my helper; I will not be afraid. What can man do to me?' " (**Hebrews 13:5–6**). How can being sure of God's love because of Jesus make a difference

when ignored by friends?

when abandoned by a parent?

when ashamed of a stupid mistake?

when dumped by a boyfriend or girlfriend?

when afflicted with a painful illness?

when moving to a new state?

THE AWKWARD TIMES

Just as three days passed between Jesus' abandonment and resurrection, we may sometimes go through an awkward time, trusting God's unfailing love before we actually see our situation change. Read **Psalm 94:14–19** and think of a time when you felt forsaken. Write your own psalm, thanking God for carrying you through that awkward time.

© 2008 Concordia Publishing House. Okay to copy.

STUDENT PAGE 48

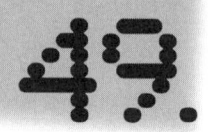

49. Something Worth Searching For

Matthew 28:1–10; John 20:1–18; Acts 10:34–43; Colossians 3:1–4

Lesson Focus

The resurrection of Jesus motivates young people to set their minds and hearts on Him as they search for meaning in their lives and share the resurrection news with others.

A SILENT SEARCH (10 minutes)

Use a pair of white gloves (your handbell director may have a pair you can borrow) to mime a sketch of someone searching for a lost and valuable item like a ring or car keys.

Ask the students to write their answers to the questions from this section on the student page. Have volunteers share their answers. In the Gospel lessons, we relive the Easter-morning search for Jesus. Today He helps us look to Him, seeing His presence with us and experiencing the way He comforts us with His love and forgiveness.

THE WORD (30 minutes)

Divide the class into two groups. Assign one group Matthew 28:1–10 and the other group John 20:1–18. Give the groups five minutes to read the account and prepare a pantomime of their stories, and then have them perform it in front of the other group. The box on the student page suggests some actions and emotions they'll want to express in their pantomime.

Discuss the question from the student page. The disciples were devastated when they buried Jesus, but now that He was alive, their hope was restored. They were no longer afraid.

Have a student read Acts 10:34–43. Have the others discuss and record an answer to the question on the student page.

Jesus knows pain; He experienced normal human pain and also endured the pain of physical beating and crucifixion. He saw the suffering of those He healed. He also knows what it's like to be abandoned by friends, made fun of, and beat up.

Read together Colossians 3:1–4. Ask students to respond to the question. Possible responses:

I don't want to get dragged back into the tomb again.

I want to stay next to Him and His Word.

I enjoy earthly things and my friends, but things break and friends sometimes hurt me or drag me down. My relationship with Jesus is the most important thing because He is always there for me.

A SEARCH SOLUTION (10 minutes)

Ask students to respond again to the questions in "A Silent Search."

CLOSING (5 minutes)

Have the class stand in a circle. In the middle of the circle, place a cross or Bible. Before you pray, ask the students to keep their eyes open and focused on the Bible or cross to symbolize their commitment to keeping their hearts and minds set on Him.

LESSON EXTENDERS

✝ Give participants paper and markers, and ask them to design a creative arrow that has the Christian commission from Acts 10 on it. Have them copy words from today's Acts text on it, cut it out, and sign their name. Display the arrows on the door to indicate that they are to go and share the Good News with the Holy Spirit's help.

Something Worth Searching For

A SILENT SEARCH

What do your friends and classmates search for in life?

Where are they looking for these things?

Even though someone doesn't ask for help, what actions tell you that person may need your friendship?

THE WORD

Read the Gospel account that was assigned to your group (**Matthew 28:1–10** or **John 20:1–18**). Prepare to pantomime this story. Include these actions:

- surprise reaction to an earthquake (Matthew account)
- fear
- seeing someone radiating (giving off the appearance of light)
- humble adoration
- going
- telling
- going someplace while it's still dark (John's account)
- Running . . . meeting someone . . . telling that person something (John's account)
- dismay
- stooping and looking
- weeping and pleading

In the Gospel accounts after the resurrection, Jesus' followers sought and searched with renewed excitement. What stirred them to these actions?

Read **Acts 10:34–43**.

How does Jesus know the hurts and struggles that you face?

Read **Colossians 3:1–4**.

How can these verses help you stay focused on Jesus and not be distracted by this world or the devil?

© 2008 Concordia Publishing House. Okay to copy.

58. Can You Believe It?

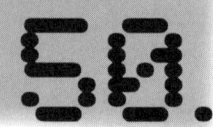

John 20:19–31

Lesson Focus

Just as Thomas doubted the reality of Jesus' resurrection, young people today are challenged for their beliefs. God's Word reassures us of the certainty of the resurrection and our eternal home in heaven.

OPENING (10 minutes)

Invite volunteers to take turns telling the class three unusual facts about themselves, two of which are true and one of which is a lie. After each person speaks, have the class vote on which fact they think is false before letting the speaker reveal the truth. If you want to keep score, give each student one point for a correct guess and subtract one point for each incorrect guess. After five or six votes ask, "Which facts could have been proved or disproved? Were there any we would have to accept on faith?"

BELIEVE IT OR NOT! (10 minutes)

Distribute copies of the student page and direct the attention of the class to the first section. Have the students write "eye" next to each subject they have seen with their own eyes, "ear" next to each one they have heard from others, and "book" next to each one they think they know to be real. Poll the class to determine if they agree on which are real and which are fictitious. Briefly discuss each subject, asking the students to explain how they might accept as truth something they haven't seen with their own eyes. Ask, "What does it take to prove the reality of what you haven't yourself experienced?"

BEYOND A DOUBT! (15 minutes)

Ask three volunteers to read the parts of Thomas, Jesus, and John the narrator, telling the story recorded in John 20:19–31. As a class, list at least three reasons Thomas had to doubt the resurrection. Possibilities include the terrible certainty of Jesus' death on the cross, Thomas's unwillingness to get his hopes up, a lack of conclusive physical evidence, Thomas's resentment that he wasn't there, or perhaps that Thomas had an analytical or rational personality. After speculating on Thomas's reasons for doubting, list at least three reasons for believing. Be sure to include the testimony of ten eyewitnesses, prior experience at the resurrection of Lazarus, and most important, Jesus' own words predicting both His death and His resurrection (Matthew 16:21; 17:22–23; 20:18–19). Encourage the students to discuss the two questions on their worksheet.

BLESS MY SOUL! (10 minutes)

Let students work in pairs to answer the questions in this section. Don't be surprised if the last question elicits some real doubts, especially from students new to Christianity. Make certain that you reassure the class that, just as Jesus loved and accepted Thomas in spite of his doubts, God loves and accepts us too.

CLOSING (5 minutes)

Bring the class back together, and invite them to read Hebrews 11:1–13 responsively. Conclude with a prayer that Christ would strengthen your faith as you wait for Him to reveal Himself at His return.

LESSON EXTENDERS

✝ Read 1 Peter 1:3–9. What results from believing in Christ without seeing Him, even during all kinds of trials?

✝ Sing a song or hymn of faith together, such as "My Faith Looks Up to Thee" (*LSB* 702).

Can You Believe It?

BELIEVE IT OR NOT!

Which of the following have you seen with your own eyes?

_ _ _ Apollo moon landings

_ _ _ Spanish-American War

_ _ _ Loch Ness monster

Which have you read about or heard of from other people?

_ _ _ Space aliens

_ _ _ Bigfoot

_ _ _ DNA

Which do you believe actually exist or really happened?

_ _ _ Subatomic particles

_ _ _ Time travel

_ _ _ Atlantis

BEYOND A DOUBT!

Read **John 20:19–31**. Put yourself in Thomas's place. In the left column, list at least three reasons to doubt the resurrection. In the right column, list at least three reasons to believe.

Reasons to Doubt   **Reasons to Believe**

....

....

....

Why do you think Thomas behaved as he did? Why do you think Jesus made a point of changing Thomas's mind?

....

....

BLESS MY SOUL!

What did Jesus mean by "blessed are those who have not seen and yet have believed" (**John 20:29**)?

....

....

How does God work through Baptism, Holy Communion, and Scripture to help us believe what we can't see?

....

....

Is there anything in God's Word you still struggle to believe? What might God think about your uncertainty?

....

....

© 2008 Concordia Publishing House. Okay to copy.

51. Mission Possible

Acts 1:1–14; John 17:1–11

Lesson Focus

Even though Jesus is no longer with us in bodily form, through the gift of the Holy Spirit each Christian is empowered to carry out the mission the Lord has called him or her to do.

I THINK I CAN
(10 minutes)

Distribute copies of the student page. Give students a few seconds to make their selections. Invite them to share their choices and the reasons behind them. Be prepared to share your choices.

CHALLENGES, CHALLENGES
(25 minutes)

Give students a minute to answer the first three questions on their own before sharing with the group. Explain that a spiritual challenge is something that tests or tempts you in your daily faith walk. Giving examples may help, such as, "My mom and I are in constant conflict. It's really hard to honor her right now."

Have students break into groups and complete the next questions under "Challenges, Challenges" and "Connecting through the Power Cord." Give students between five and ten minutes in their groups. Have one person from each group share that group's answers.

Jesus told the disciples that they would be His witnesses locally and to the ends of the earth.

The disciples had been involved in ministry already, with Jesus on location to guide them. Immediately after He instructed the disciples to witness to the ends of the earth, He ascended—leaving them to do things on their own.

In order to carry out their work, the disciples needed the Holy Spirit. Jesus instructed them to wait for the Holy Spirit before they set out (vv. 4–5). It is only by the power of the Holy Spirit through the Word and Sacraments that faith is worked in people's hearts.

CONNECTING THROUGH THE POWER CORD
(5 minutes)

Jesus prayed and taught the disciples to pray. The disciples prayed constantly with other believers.

Jesus prayed prior to His arrest. (He also alludes to His ascension in v. 11.)

Prayer, both alone and together with others, is a precious gift from God. God promises to hear and answer prayer.

PLUGGED IN
(10 minutes)

Read the paragraph together and discuss the question. Emphasize the importance of God's gift of prayer and the power of the Holy Spirit to carry out our tasks. Pray: "Dear Lord, thank You for the gift of the Holy Spirit. Help each of us stay connected to You through prayer. Amen."

LESSON EXTENDERS

✝ Institute a prayer-partners program within your group. Set aside time regularly for the partners to pray together.

✝ List the steps suggested in discussion of the final question for the group to see. During the next class session, encourage students to share stories of how the steps helped them face their challenges.

Mission Possible

I THINK I CAN
Place a star by the challenge you would like most to face by yourself. Place an X by the one you would find most difficult.

_____ Three days of wilderness hiking

_____ Cooking a gourmet dinner for four

_____ Balancing a checkbook

_____ Writing an original play

CHALLENGES, CHALLENGES
What is the greatest spiritual challenge you currently face?

What is the greatest spiritual challenge you can imagine facing?

What would give you the courage to meet these challenges?

Read **Acts 1:1–14**.

1. What challenge did Jesus put before the disciples (**v. 8**)?

2. Why might this have seemed overwhelming compared to what they had been doing (**v. 9**)?

3. What did they need before they would be able to meet that challenge (**vv. 5, 8**)?

CONNECTING THROUGH THE POWER CORD
In **Acts 1:14**, what did the disciples spend their time doing while waiting for the Holy Spirit?

Read **John 17:1–11**.

1. What was Jesus busy doing in these verses?

2. What can we learn through the examples of Jesus and the disciples in these sections of Scripture?

PLUGGED IN
The disciples were faced with the huge task of spreading the Gospel throughout the world. The task seemed even more overwhelming because Jesus ascended to heaven, leaving the disciples alone to do their task. Then He sent the Holy Spirit to give them power. God promises that we are always connected to Him. We are never alone. He gives us power and strength.

When you are feeling alone, what steps can you take to overcome the challenges you face?

© 2008 Concordia Publishing House. Okay to copy.

STUDENT PAGE 51

52. WHAT DID YOU SAY?

Acts 2:1–41;
Joel 2:28–29;
John 16:5–11

Lesson Focus

The Holy Spirit continues to empower our relationship with God by helping us to gladly hear and understand God's Word.

SAY WHAT? (10 minutes)

Distribute copies of the student page. Ask students to think about the way they talk. Do they sometimes slip into slang? Do they use a lot of "verbal garbage" ("er," "you know," "um," "like," "ah")? What does the expression "huh?" mean? When or why is it used?

HUH? (15 minutes)

Students may need help to understand about the Holy Spirit. People two thousand years ago didn't get it, either. Peter tried to explain after some of the crowd mocked the disciples.

Read the Bible passages and discuss the questions. Suggested responses:

Some people suggested that the disciples were drunk.

Joel spoke of a time when the Holy Spirit would rest upon all people, not just the prophets.

Peter pled his case by speaking of the death and resurrection of Christ. Peter talked about David, who was respected by Peter's audience and who looked forward to the Messiah.

The people began to listen when their hearts were touched; God's Word caused repentance and desire for God's forgiveness.

After Peter heard and saw how God's Word had touched the people, he proclaimed the gift of God's grace that comes through Baptism.

The people gladly received the Word and were baptized.

LISTEN UP (20 minutes)

Have the class read John 16:5–11. The Holy Spirit acts to counsel us in our faith (i.e., to produce, enable, and grow faith within us).

The Holy Spirit encourages us in our faith, helps us learn and understand God's Word, helps us make sense of God's Law and Gospel, sustains our relationship with God, and gives us courage to live out our faith.

Ask students if listening or speaking is more important. How and when can either action be taken for granted?

Ask students to reflect about their lives. When are they silent? What are they saying when they open their mouths?

What is the role of our tongue in our relationship with God? How can our mouths be used to serve Him?

When can they be a coach, teacher, helper, lawyer, or friend for Christ?

CLOSING (5 minutes)

Close in prayer, asking God to guide the students as they speak and listen. Be sure to include any specific prayer requests that students may have.

LESSON EXTENDERS

✝ Ask students to keep a one-week record of what they say (what, when, where, how, and to whom). Does their tongue increase their sense of marvel, closeness, distance, and/or conflict in relationship with others?

What Did You Say?

SAY WHAT?

Have you ever tried counting how many times you've said "huh?" or "what?" in a single day? Did you just say "huh?" when you read the last sentence? "Huh?" is a request for clarification, an essential part of completing the communication loop. If it were not for the vitally important "Huh?" we would often be left in the dark or unable to function. "Huh?" is difficult to live without. In what circumstances do you say it more often?

_____ With teachers?
_____ With friends?
_____ With siblings?
_____ With parents?
_____ With grandparents?
_____ With relatives?

HUH?

Imagine the possibility of being so "with it" that you see God's promise being fulfilled right before your eyes! What thoughts might be going through your head?

Read **Acts 2:1–12**.

The people were amazed and confused. How were the disciples mocked (**v. 13**)?

What did Peter mean when he stood up and explained that they all had witnessed the fulfillment of the prophet Joel (**vv. 14–21**)?

What else did Peter say in response (**vv. 22–24**)? How was the history of God's people important to this message (**vv. 25–36**)?

How did the people respond (**vv. 36–37**)?

What did Peter proclaim about the way God works to save repentant sinners (**vv. 38–40**)?

How did the people respond (**v. 41**)?

LISTEN UP

The Holy Spirit is also referred to as the Comforter. A comforter listens to you and cares for you deeply.

Read **John 16:5–11**.

What is the job of the Holy Spirit in **verse 7**?

How is the Spirit like a coach? teacher? lawyer? friend? helper?

© 2008 Concordia Publishing House. Okay to copy.

STUDENT PAGE 52